Saint Monica
and
Her Son Augustine

Saint Monica
and
Her Son Augustine

(331-387)

by
Leon Cristiani

Translated from the French by
M. Angeline Bouchard

BOOKS & MEDIA
BOSTON

Imprimatur: ✠ Humberto Cardinal Medeiros
Archbishop of Boston
February 17, 1977
Original French title: *Sainte Monique*
Nihil Obstat: Jean Gautier, PSS
Imprimatur: J. Le Cordier, VG

Title of first English edition: *The Story of St. Monica and
Her Son Augustine*
Second edition: 1994
Cover Art: Giraudon / Art Resource, NY Lauros. SCHEFFER,
Ary. Fr. (1795-1858) Saint Augustine et Sainte
Monique. Paris, Louvre, France.

Library of Congress Cataloging-in-Publication Data

[Sainte Monique, 331-387. English]
Saint Monica and her son Augustine (331-387) / by Leon Cristiani;
translated from the French by M. Angeline Bouchard.
p.   cm.
Originally published in English as The story of Monica and her son
Augustine (331-387). 1975.
ISBN 0-8198-0462-2
1. Monica, Saint, d. 387. I. Title.
BR1710.C7513   1994
270.2'092—dc20
[B]   94-27903
CIP

Printed and published in the U.S.A. by Pauline Books & Media,
50 Saint Pauls Avenue, Boston MA 02130-3491.

www.pauline.org

Pauline Books & Media is the publishing house of the Daughters of St.
Paul, an international congregation of women religious serving the
Church with the communications media.

7 8 9 10 11 12 13   08 07 06 05 04 03

Contents

Foreword

Everything about great men and women, everything that ever happened to them is a matter of interest to posterity. We like to expatiate on the places where they lived, the historical epoch when they reached the apex of their powers, the blood that flowed in their veins. We inquire into their lineage and the various families that contributed to the flowering of these rare and magnificent human beings.

This holds true, of course, for all whom history has ranked among the very great. There are certain instances, however, when the life of one of these famous persons has been closely linked with members of his or her family or entourage. This is the case with St. Monica. She is certainly a saint in her own right. In addition, it was through her that her son came to accept the Catholic Faith and then became a saint. This was Augustine, one of the greatest geniuses the world has known.

The names of Monica and Augustine are inseparable. We cannot think of the mother without thinking also of her son. He is the principal reason why she has been known to later generations. And without her, he would not have become the man whom history still acclaims. He was the first to declare that she had had as much pain bringing him

11

forth to the Christian Faith as when she bore him as an infant. She was not content to bring him into the world. She did not rest until she had given him to Christ and to His Church.

As we know, Monica said that after she had brought Augustine to the baptismal font, her task was over. She no longer wanted anything of earthly life. She was ready to die and await in heaven the one for whom she had wept so bitterly when he was still sunk in error and carnal pleasures.

Without Monica we would not have Augustine. We venerate her in great part because she gave him to the world. Hence it will not even be possible to write her biography without talking a great deal about Augustine. Fidelity to historical fact demands that we present two saints, showing the many close bonds that joined them throughout their lives. This was clearly seen by the principal, and almost the only French biographer of St. Monica: Abbé Louis Victor Emile Bougaud, born in Dijon in 1823, and who was the bishop of Laval, France, when he died in 1888.[1]

Abbé Bougaud was the vicar-general for Bishop Dupanloup of Orleans when he published the first edition of his *Histoire de Sainte Monique* in 1866. He rightfully claimed to be the first person to write her biography. To quote him: "No one has yet thought of giving us the story of St. Monica." When he talked of doing it, his friends seemed "a bit surprised and worried." Why were they concerned? Because everyone knew there were very few sources from which to draw on for such a biography. Indeed, what do we know about Monica? Only what St. Augustine has told us personally in his immortal *Confessions*, or through allusions he may have made to her in a few of his other writings or sermons. To these sources Abbé Bougaud did not hesitate to add the sparse references to Monica to be found in

---

1. Translator calls attention to a work by L. André-Delastre, entitled *Sainte Monique*, published in Lyons, France, 1960.

the breviaries then used by various communities of the Canons or hermits of St. Augustine.

We shall follow the example of Abbé Bougaud, but with a little more critical reserve. We shall be very careful to set apart in a special way whatever comes to us directly from Augustine. For that is inviolable from the point of view of history; that alone is absolutely reliable. But the few nuggets we can discover in the lessons of the Augustinian breviaries will fit in so well with the logic of things, that we shall have no scruples in including them in our account.

Abbé Bougaud's biography of St. Monica was a great success. He wrote with elegance and ease. It is a pleasure to read what he has to say. However, we feel that a few of his pages are too flowery and declamatory for present tastes. He began the book with an *Introduction* on the wonderful power Providence has bestowed upon mothers to obtain their children's salvation. This passage of his book actually made many mothers weep. In fact, one of them was so much impressed that she obtained permission to print 100,000 copies of this *Introduction* "in order to bring to many other mothers the consolation she herself had derived from it."

Actually, Abbé Bougaud set out to write the biography of St. Monica as a tribute to her sufferings and tears as a mother. He approached these sufferings with real enthusiasm, writing in accents that touched many hearts in his own day.

Although we live in a much less romantic age than he, we shall repeat what he said then:

"A story like the one I am about to tell should not be written. It should be sung, for it is a poem. It is the poem of the most beautiful of all loves, the deepest and most tender of loves, the loftiest and purest, also the strongest, the most patient, and the most invincible. It is a love that survived twenty-five years of trials and tears without wavering for an instant, but rather grew with trials, becoming more fervent and unwavering in proportion to the obstacles it encountered. A love that finally triumphed—for who could resist such a love?—and ended in ecstasy."

In his *Introduction,* Abbé Bougaud went on to cite other Christian mothers whose maternal love was as intense and pure as Monica's, indeed, some of whom even preferred to see their children die rather than be sullied by sin and dishonor.

Who can forget the mothers of St. Basil and St. Gregory of Nyssa, of St. John Chrysostom, St. Bernard of Clairvaux, and so many others? How can we separate St. Louis of France from Blanche of Castille? And even in the Old Testament, we read the words of a mother to her youngest son:

"Son, have pity on me, who carried you in my womb for nine months, nursed you for three years, brought you up, educated and supported you.... I beg you, child,...do not be afraid of this executioner, but be worthy of your [six] brothers and accept death, so that in the time of mercy I may receive you again with them" (2 Maccabees 7:27-29).

We therefore conclude in the words of Abbé Bougaud:

"Read the story of St. Monica. Let this wife and mother teach you to pray and to weep, to hope always, and never grow discouraged. And do not forget that so many young men are threatened by great dangers today because their wives and mothers have not wept and prayed enough for them."

Introduction

This is a fascinating true story that could have happened right here and now in the U.S.A. instead of in North Africa and Italy during the fourth century A.D. As we read it we grapple with many of the problems facing parents and children today, and see how one woman overcame them through her generous love and her faith in God. Every woman who has ever worried and prayed over her husband and children can find hope and solace in Monica's example.

The fact remains that Monica and Augustine were extraordinary people. What mother would not be proud to claim the great Augustine as her son? A man of rare genius, destined to be a saint. Not a ready-made saint, but one who fought his way slowly out of his carnal passions to perfect chastity, who sank from error to error before finding the lodestar of divinely revealed Truth. And finally a man who emerged from the infernal isolation of egoism, sin, and irreligion into the incomparable fellowship of God-Trinity.

Throughout Augustine's struggle, Monica was watching and praying. She early discovered that being the mother of such a son was rigorously demanding. It was to take all her natural resources of mind and heart, of which she had an ample supply, plus the supernatural gifts of divine grace, to bring her son to the safe haven of God's all-embracing love.

As we read Monica's biography, we may find that the author has tended to idealize her at times. From the point of view of modern psychology, perhaps she was too protective, thereby eliciting reactions of rebellion in her son. But in the end her influence on him was for the good. Women can learn from her that unceasing, fervent prayer to God for their loved ones will be heard—perhaps not as quickly as they would hope, or in the way they had hoped, but in God's own good time and way, which is, after all, the best.

A quarrel that had good results

*I*t happened in the year of our Lord 347 or 348 in the little town of Tagaste in Numidia, North Africa. A quarrel had broken out between two young women and their angry words resounded. One of them, a young girl belonging to an upper-class family, was castigating a maidservant. What were they quarreling about? Our sources do not tell us. But we know how the quarrel ended.

It seems that the servant girl, doubtless a slave as was the custom at that time, could find no more effective argument against her young mistress than to fling at her one of the most humiliating insults possible for a well-born young lady brought up in the Roman tradition. She shouted at Monica: "You bibber of pure wine!" Nowadays, she would have said: "You alcoholic!"

1

Monica's Childhood and Youth

The young mistress blushed and was silent. Tears rushed to her eyes. She was honest enough to admit to herself that the slave had spoken the truth. So brave and resolute was her character that she immediately swore to overcome her failing. This quarrel was a turning point in her life, the signal for a genuine conversion.

There is so little to this story that one almost hesitates to tell it. And yet, let us think about it. How has it come to us? Through Augustine's personal testimony in his *Confessions*. And how did he learn of it? Most probably from his mother. So it appears the slave's taunt had hit the mark. Later on, when Monica was training her son, she liked to tell him how easy it is to fall into vice almost without realizing it, how necessary it is to fight against one's weaknesses as soon as we discover them, how truth can come from the lips of an irate servant, and how we must learn to accept the truth even in such circumstances as coming from God Himself who is Truth.

But let us come back to Monica's family background.

At Tagaste

Monica was born in Tagaste, a small and relatively unknown town of North Africa in what is now Tunisia, unmentioned by any of the ancient authors except Pliny. In modern times Tagaste is known as *Souk-Ahras*, and is located about halfway between Carthage and Hippo, that is, between Tunis and Bone. Augustine has told us that his mother died shortly after he was baptized, in her fifty-sixth year, in 387. We can therefore assume she was born in the year 331.

Monica came from a prominent family, as we can judge from the rank of her husband who was one of the leaders of the city. She was born of Christian parents, and if we are to believe the Augustinian breviaries, her mother's name was *Facunda* or *Facundia*. Although Monica received her name at birth, according to her own account, she was not baptized until she was seventeen or eighteen. It seems that hers was the only family that had not succumbed to the Donatist schism that first appeared early in the fourth century and was to tear Christian Africa apart for many years.

However, about the year 348 or 349 an imperial law promulgated by Constans I, one of Constantine's sons, severely condemned the excesses of the Donatist sect. As a consequence, the entire town of Tagaste renounced the schism and rallied to Catholic unity. It has been conjectured that it was about this time, and perhaps as a result of the town's return to orthodoxy, that Monica was baptized.

As was the custom, Monica had begun her education in the Christian Faith long before. She had a very old grandmother who had lived through the age of the martyrs. Monica spent many hours at her feet. The old lady used to tell her about the past of the Christian Church in Africa, and lingered over the inspiring or tragic scenes she had witnessed. We can reconstruct at least some parts of the most beautiful stories Monica's grandmother told her.

It was by way of Carthage that the Christian Faith had come to Africa, although we have no way of knowing exactly when. Around the year 180 A.D., two groups of martyrs had nobly confessed their faith. First, there were the martyrs of Scilli; and then there were the martyrs of Madaura, a town close to Tagaste. In or about the year 203, two admirable women, Perpetua and Felicitas, gave their lives for Christ. In the fourth century North Africans were still reading the account of their witness, written in part by Perpetua herself.

During the same period, Africa had an eminent doctor of Christian teaching, the great Tertullian. Toward the middle of the third century, another doctor—who was also a very great bishop and a glorious martyr—gave glory to Carthage: St. Cyprian. There were other well-known martyrs like Sts. James and Marian, Montanus and Lucius, all of whom died in the year 259. Likewise Sts. Marcellus and Cassian, the aged Tipasius who died in 298, as well as the holy martyrs Saturninus and Dativus, who died in 304. Another woman martyr, St. Salsa, died for Christ at a time still closer to Monica's own.

Unquestionably, the little girl's faith was kindled by the stories of these martyrs, and it was to remain invincible throughout her life. It is hard for us to conceive of the enthusiasm and firm resolve that such examples of heroism inspired among the Christian men and women of that day. Augustine's great care in later years to speak of the African martyrs in his sermons at Hippo is good proof of the vigor with which Christian traditions were preserved.

Monica certainly must have grown up in this atmosphere of Christian heroism. When she went to live in Milan, Italy, as a matron, during the time of the Arian threats to the Faith, she was among the most ardent supporters of Bishop St. Ambrose, in her yearning to suffer martyrdom for Jesus Christ.

Not only did Monica remember the instruction given her by her mother and the stories she had heard from her grandmother. When she spoke to her son Augustine about her girlhood, she always mentioned the austere and elderly woman-servant to whose care she had often been entrusted. This slave was considered a member of the family. She was treated not as a servant but as a friend of the household, indeed, as a close relative. She had been the nurse of Monica's father when he was a child, and had carried him on her shoulders "the way young mothers carry their small children," Augustine tells us. She had been present at his wedding. Treated with veneration and honor, she took care of the second generation of children as well as the first. We can picture her as trustworthy, prudent, with a tendency to scold, but full of maternal dedication. To quote St. Augustine once more:

"...she was given charge of her master's daughters. This charge she fulfilled most conscientiously, checking them sharply when necessary with holy severity and teaching them soberly and prudently. Thus, except at the times when they ate—and that most temperately—at their parents' table, she would not let them even drink water, no matter how tormenting their thirst. By this she prevented the forming of a bad habit, and she used to remark very sensibly: 'Now you drink water because you are not allowed to have wine; but when you are married, and thus mistresses of food-stores and wine-cellars, you will despise water, but the habit of drinking will still remain.'"[1]

Monica may have thought her nurse was far too strict. However, by such training she developed the eminent virtues that were to have such a prodigious influence on the genius-son God had in store for her.

In any event, we can be sure that the training received from the "decrepit" old servant, as Augustine called her, came to Monica's mind in the heat of the quarrel we related earlier in this chapter.

The birth of a vice

The little girl grew to adolescence. The old slave had died, faithful to the end. She had trained Monica so well that her parents decided to initiate her into the duties of running a home. One of these duties was to go down to the wine-cellar every day to get the supply of wine needed for the family meal.

---

1. *The Confessions of St. Augustine*, Book Nine, VIII, translated by F. J. Sheed (New York: Sheed and Ward, 1943), p. 195. All subsequent quotations from *The Confessions...* for which a page number is given are taken from this edition.

She was known to be so well-behaved and on her guard against the dangers of wine that no one in the house had any qualms about entrusting her with this task. Let us listen to Augustine relate what she herself must have told him many times during his childhood:

"For when...she was sent by her parents...to draw wine from the barrel, she would dip the cup in, but before pouring the wine from the cup into the flagon, she would sip a little with the very tip of her lips, only a little because she did not yet like the taste sufficiently to take more. Indeed she did it not out of any craving for wine, but rather from the excess of childhood's high spirits, which tend to boil over in absurdities, and are usually kept in check by the authority of elders. And so, adding to that daily drop a little more from day to day — for he that despises small things, falls little by little — she fell into the habit, so that she would drink off greedily cups almost full of wine" (*Confessions*, Book Nine, VIII, p. 196).

When Augustine tells this story, he is filled with emotion. Obviously he is reminded of his own youth. His mother had so often warned him against the far too easy descent from minor infractions into the most serious sins.

"Where then was that wise old woman with her forceful prohibitions? Could anything avail against the evil in us, unless Your healing, O Lord, watched over us?" (*Confessions, ibid.*)

And then he goes into raptures on the winding paths divine grace uses when it wants to touch a soul. Drawing from his own experience, he continues:

"When our father and mother and nurses are absent, You are present, who created us, who call us, who can use those placed over us for some good unto the salvation of our souls. What did You do then, O my God? How did You cure her, and bring her to health?" (*Confessions, ibid.*)

We can be sure that Augustine's words faithfully echo Monica's thoughts. When Monica recalled her senseless quarrel with the young servant girl, the insult the latter hurled at her, and her own resolve to overcome her nascent vice, she instinctively admitted that God Himself had so arranged it all to save her from the abyss of danger over which she was teetering.

In the words of Augustine:

"A maidservant with whom she was accustomed to go to the cellar, one day fell into a quarrel with her small mistress when no one else chanced to be about" (*Confessions, ibid.*).

This slave was the instrument God chose to reprove Monica. For she retorted to Monica's chiding by calling her a *meribibulam*, that is, a bibber of pure wine, a drunkard—or as we now say, an alcoholic.

This was enough to change the course of Monica's whole life. She was a profoundly religious girl, nurtured in the best traditions of Africa's Christian heritage. Besides, she had been warned repeatedly by her old nurse against the vice that now threatened to take possession of her. And so the accusation was not lost on her.

Augustine concludes:

"My mother was pierced to the quick, saw her fault in its true wickedness, and instantly condemned it and gave it up. Just as the flattery of a friend can pervert, so the insult of an enemy can sometimes correct. Nor do You, O God, reward men according to what You do by means of them, but according to what they themselves intended. For the girl, being in a temper, wanted to enrage her young mistress, not to amend her, for she did it when no one else was there, either because the time and place happened to be thus when the quarrel arose, or because she was afraid that elders would be angry because she had not told it sooner. But You, O Lord, Ruler of heavenly things and earthly, who turn to Your own purposes the very depths of rivers as they run and order the turbulence of the flow of time, did by the folly of one mind bring sanity to another; thus reminding us not to attribute it to our own power if another is amended by our word, even if we meant to amend him" (*Confessions*, Book Nine, VIII, pp. 196-197).

Such was the almost trivial simplicity of Monica's spiritual crisis. She became humbler, less self-confident, more given to mortification. And in this way she was preparing herself unknowingly for the great tasks that would be hers when she trained her own children.

Monica's piety

What we should remember about this episode, and especially about Augustine's commentaries on it, is that nothing that happens to us in our lives is useless. For divine Providence is always at work within us. That is the deepest meaning of Christ's words: *"Every hair of your head has been counted!"* (Matthew 10:30) Now, a single hair is a very small thing. But God knows how many hairs we have on our heads, and not one falls without His permission. Augustine was to be thoroughly convinced of this after he had achieved his own conversion.

While Augustine must have discovered this truth in the Gospels and the Epistles of St. Paul, which he read and meditated upon so carefully, we can also be sure he had first learned it as a small child at his mother's knee. For Monica's devotion consisted precisely in the oldest and most reliable form of Christian spirituality, which consists in believing that God governs all things and is present everywhere, that we must constantly pray to Him and continually carry on a loving conversation with Him.

We can profitably seek information from the Augustinian breviaries on Monica's habitual Christian practices as a young girl. They all agree on this point. As we have already said, according to the customs of the time, Monica was probably not baptized until she was seventeen or eighteen years old. This does not mean she had not attended church from her earliest childhood. In fact, she had taken delight in doing so. The lessons in the breviaries assure us that even when she was a tiny girl she took advantage of moments when no one was watching her to slip away to church. There she would talk to God in her childish way, and all but forget to return home. One text culled by the Bollandists[2] for May 4, the traditional feast day of St. Monica, affirms that when she came home she was severely scolded and sometimes even beaten. But neither reprimands nor punishments could wrest a word of complaint from her.

At other times, in the midst of a game with her companions, she would be found motionless and recollected, deep in prayer at the foot of a tree. And even during the night she would often get up secretly, fall on her knees and join her hands while reciting the few prayers she knew. One of these must have been the Lord's Prayer, then the most widely used Christian prayer, which her mother and nurse had taught her.

We know that in later years Monica was to be one of the most assiduous devotees of prayer around Bishop Ambrose of Milan. So it would seem that the notations in the breviaries about her early prayer life are probably correct. Who can doubt that Monica developed in early childhood the love of prayer so evident during her mature years, that was to be her

---

2. The Bollandists were "a small group of Jesuits in Antwerp, Belgium, organized into a society in the seventeenth century by Jean Bolland for the critical study and publication of the lives of the saints" (New Catholic Encyclopedia, Volume 2, p. 648).

strength and hope amid the great trials of her life as wife and mother?

Monica's personality

It is a law of God's *modus operandi* towards souls that He engrafts His loftiest supernatural gifts upon the qualities of nature. And that is readily understandable, since God is the Author of nature, quite as much as of supernature. Monica certainly had very exceptional qualities in the natural order. Her son Augustine, speaking with no intention of mutilating the truth, said that her intuitive and penetrating intellect was on the borderline of genius. She understood the lofty speculations of the philosophers and theologians to the point of being able to express luminous and pertinent views in discussions or conversations on the most abstruse and sublime subjects. Augustine even goes so far as to say that he and his friends used to sit around her listening breathlessly as she spoke, *"as though they were listening to some great man"* in their midst. Monica had an insatiable thirst to learn and to understand. But needless to say, she was outstanding far more because of her gifts of heart and will than those of the intellect.

Monica was blessed with an even temper, patience beyond compare, wonderful discernment, as well as admirable perseverance in her resolutions. Hers was a richly endowed personality in the fullest sense of the word. From the physical point of view, we know nothing about her appearance. Was she tall or short, a woman of great beauty? We do not know. However, it is hard to believe that some reflections of her inward beauty, especially her kindness and great gentleness, should not have appeared outwardly and impressed those who saw her. A text culled by the Bollandists affirms that she rejected the use of superfluous ornaments, preferring the simplicity and modesty in attire so eloquently praised by St. Cyprian, the great doctor of Africa.

All in all, we like to think that Monica was an accomplished young lady from every point of view, and that in all things she glorified the God whose love she carried within her great heart.

Monica's marriage

Monica's parents were proud of their daughter, and must have begun thinking of marrying her off at an early age. At that time and for many centuries afterward, marriage was the parents' concern, perhaps even more than the choice of the principal interested parties. It was the parents who chose their future son-in-law. Even St. Paul, in speaking about young girls, intimated that it was their fathers who decided whom they were to marry and what their fate would be.

After all we have said about Monica's qualities, it is all the more surprising that her parents chose to marry her to a man who was to cause her so much suffering, unless we are to admit that she had been specifically predestined to win for Christ, by her gentleness, patience, and chastity, a man who was as far removed from the Christian Faith as can be imagined.

The man's name was Patricius. He seems to have held a position of some importance in Tagaste. Actually, he was one of the decurions, that is, municipal· magistrates. This title was given only to the most outstanding landowners of the city. Actually, even at that time, it involved more disadvantages than advantages. The imperial treasury, always eager for money, had decided to entrust to the decurions the collection, and especially the supervision of the taxes in their city. This meant that the decurions or *curiales* were obliged to make up from their own funds the sum due the Roman treasury by the city, in the event they could not get their less fortunate compatriots to pay their taxes.

Nevertheless, the title of *curiale* gave a certain authority to the man who bore it. From this point of view, therefore, Patricius was what might be called "a good catch."

And yet Monica's parents could well have entertained very serious objections to such a choice. In the first place, Patricius was a pagan. There were still quite a number of pagans among the Christianized populations. For a devout Christian girl, marriage to an unbeliever could only be a matter of deep sorrow. Besides, Patricius was much older than she. It is not recorded whether he had been married previously. In any case he had no children, even if he had been married. For Monica would have taken charge of them in marrying Patricius and we would have known about it. Be this as it may, Patricius must have been about 55 years old when he married Monica, and she was then 22. Thirty-three years is a great difference in age! On the basis of age alone, this could prove to be a mismatch.

Finally, Patricius does not seem to have been a man of greater chastity than the average pagan of his time. Although he had decided to take a wife, he had no intention of renouncing his earlier more or less hidden and sordid sexual relationships.

This was to cause Monica much suffering and humiliation, and many secret tears. Augustine's revelations have given us a hint of these things.

But for all his faults and even his vices, Patricius also had good qualities. His son Augustine assures us that he had a generous heart, and that helps to forgive many things.

In any event, Monica obeyed her parents and pledged her faith to this man. They were married, probably in the year 353, as we have said. Now we shall see what kind of a wife Monica became, before turning to her role as a mother.

Texts by Tertullian

*L*et us try to understand the nature of the difficulties Monica encountered upon entering the home of her pagan husband. Perhaps no one has written more eloquently on the subject of marriage between Christians and pagans than Tertullian. It is quite possible that Monica had actually read Tertullian, a Christian author who had lived in Africa. Indeed, he was one of the glories of the youthful Christian literature, and St. Cyprian used to call him his "master."

In his famous treatise *Ad Uxorem* (To a Wife), Tertullian contrasted the happiness of spouses united in the same faith and in the worship of the one true God with the marital difficulties of those separated by diversity of religious belief.

To quote Tertullian: "How can a Christian woman serve God, if her husband does not worship Him? If she has to go to church, he will insist on meeting her at the baths earlier than

2

Monica, the Wife

usual. If it is time for her to fast, he will order a great
feast for that very day. If she has to go out, the servants will be too busy with many duties to allow it.
...Will this husband allow his wife to visit her Christian brothers in the hovels of the poor? Will he tol-
erate that she should get up in the middle of the night
to take part in the Paschal solemnities? Will he permit
her to receive Holy Communion when the pagans
say so many terrible things about it? Will he think it
good that she should slip into prisons to kiss the
chains of confessors of the faith, to wash the feet of
the saints? If there is call to give something to passing strangers, to travelers, to the needy, even the
attic and the cellar will be closed up tight!..."

Tertullian must have been describing condi-
tions that he witnessed personally. In his view, any
marriage not based on community of religion and
moral ideals rested on shaky foundations. And the
great writer did not forget to point out still another
peril. For a pagan husband, there are entirely different social duties than for Christian fellowship. He
will want his wife to accompany him in all the places
he is accustomed to frequent.

Then Tertullian asks: "Will not the Christian
wife be urged by her pagan husband to take on some
of the ways of the pagan woman? Will she not be
obliged for her husband's sake to cultivate her beauty,
wear ornaments, take meticulous care of her body,
and practice a lack of restraint that God does not
bless?"

How different is the picture of truly Christian
spouses! If Monica had read pages such as this, there
can be no doubt that she went over them many times
in her mind during the eighteen years of her marriage
to Patricius.

Monica's conjugal strategy

If Monica was tempted to lose heart when she
became the wife of a man like Patricius, she bravely

overcame the temptation. It mattered not that Patricius was still a pagan, accustomed to the most vulgar and unchristian pleasures, and reputed to be a violent and brutal man. Augustine bears witness that she overcame her ever-recurring discouragement. Her courage in these circumstances is magnificent proof of her faith in God. But to understand all this we must look closely at what the *Confessions* have to say.

Augustine has given us a brief description of what we might call Monica's "conjugal strategy." We have already pointed out that she was a very intelligent woman. In this instance, her intelligence, with the help of faith, helped her to see clearly the goal to be attained as well as the means to be used.

From the start she set herself a great and beautiful goal: she would win her husband for Christ. In this, she offers an immortal example to all Christian wives. She wanted the salvation of the man to whom she was joined by the bonds of marriage and who was to be the father of her children. To this end she realized she must treat him first of all as a husband, showing him the deference and obedience that marriage called for. Under Roman law, the husband had all the rights, so to speak. The wife was not considered to be the husband's equal, but rather a child, as it were, in his power — "in his hand," as the saying was.

Yet Monica hoped to win this ingrained pagan to the Christian Faith. And this she planned to achieve by her docility and submission, but even more by the slow and imperceptible impact of her virtues, her gentleness, her moral dignity and selflessness.

In his *Confessions*, St. Augustine has told us so quite clearly:

"My mother, then, was modestly and soberly brought up, being rather made obedient to her parents by You than to You by her parents. When she reached the age for marriage, and was bestowed upon a husband, she served him as her lord. She used all her effort to win him to You, preaching You to him by her character, by which You made her beautiful to her husband, respected and loved by him and admirable in his sight" (*Confessions*, Book Nine, IX, p. 197).

We understand this to mean that she did not use verbal debate, she did not try to "catechize" a husband who was much older than she and completely unresponsive. She did not chide or remonstrate, or deliver tiresome and useless sermons. Instead, she used gentleness, forthrightness, simplicity, fidelity, modesty, great dignity of manner and language, impeccable behavior — without ostentation or affectation, but with untiring discretion.

We have called Monica's method her "conjugal strategy." It was a strategy founded on prayer, faith, and on love far superior to the love of the senses. It was a strategy of rare power which proved the only effective one in the end. It was to take her a long time, but she did attain her goal. Her husband finally surrendered. He died a Christian and received baptism on his deathbed at his own request.

Monica's strategy in practice

Monica had a plan of action not based on selfish motives or her own interest; it was born of lofty desires rather than carefully thought-out and methodical reflection. In a word, she obeyed the interior voice of her God. She acted like a true Christian woman, and sought her everyday inspirations in continual prayer. She was counting on God alone and not on her own personal efforts. This is clearly evident from what her son Augustine tells us about her life as a wife. He could remember many things himself, since he was at least seventeen years old when his father died. Being a very precocious youth, he understood many happenings that he later reduced to writing. And he

must have talked about them more than once with his
mother, whom he deeply revered.

The first point he makes, indeed the most delicate
of all, concerns her attitude toward his father's mis-
conduct.

He reported this categorically, briefly, and
adequately:

"She bore his acts of unfaithfulness quietly, and
never had any jealous scene with her husband about
them" (*Confessions,* Book Nine, IX, p. 197).

She knew, she saw, but she kept quiet and suffered in silence. She prayed, and probably wept, but
she realized that the religion of the pagans condoned
great moral degradation in the matter of sexual relations. In her heart, she contrasted the demands of
the Christian Faith with the laxity of the pagans. She
waited for her husband's heart to be won to faith, so
that he might also be won over to the practice of conjugal fidelity.

Continuing his dialogue with God, as he does
throughout his *Confessions,* Augustine says:

"She awaited Your mercy upon him, that he might
grow chaste through faith in You" (*Confessions,*
Book Nine, IX, p. 197).

At this point, it might be well to point out that the
word *Confessions,* as used by Augustine, does not
mean the admission of sins, but *Praises to God.*

Monica waited many long years, and this, too,
is an example for so many Christian wives who have
in every age been faced with the same problem.

But Patricius was not only a philandering husband. He was also a violent man, prone to anger. We
are told this type of temperament was quite common
among the Africans. Augustine says that Patricius was
a *"violent husband,"* which we can interpret to mean
rough and brutal. He lost his temper easily, and at
such times showed himself to be a glowering and
terrifying man. This was a common occurrence at
Tagaste. Many a young wife had to hold her own

against a fractious and aggressive husband. We learn this from Augustine, too, speaking of his mother.

What did Monica do in the face of her husband's anger? Her favorite weapon was patience. She said nothing. She waited until the fit of anger was over. She found a way of restoring her husband's composure after the storm. We know he was a very generous man. In the end, he always understood. And his wife's behavior toward him was no doubt one of the most convincing proofs of the truth of her faith in Jesus Christ. To quote Augustine again:

"But she knew that a woman must not resist a husband in anger, by deed or even by word. Only, when she saw him calm again and quiet, she would take the opportunity to give him an explanation of her actions..." (*Confessions*, Book Nine, IX, p. 197).

Monica's method of handling her husband was so successful that the married women of Tagaste used to talk about it when they gathered together. Actually, according to Augustine, "many matrons with much milder husbands 'carried the marks of blows to disfigure their faces, and would all get together to complain of the way their husbands behaved" (*Confessions*, Book Nine, IX, p. 197). So it seems that most marriages in Tagaste were subject to severe marital troubles. The poor wives were often beaten! When they complained to Monica, she wittily "advised them against their tongues." And yet they all knew that Patricius was not easy to get along with. Nonetheless, "it had never been heard, and there was no mark to show, that Patricius had beaten his wife or that there had been any family quarrel between them for so much as a single day" (*Confessions*, Book Nine, IX, pp. 197-198).

This was a kind of miracle that was talked about in the little town of Tagaste and was part of the chronicles of its daily events.

The children

The fact remains that if Monica had not given Patricius beautiful children, neither her discretion, nor her dignity as a faithful wife, nor her patience and gentleness would have overcome his inveterate paganism. But she bore him children. In the next chapter we shall talk about Augustine, and what he meant to Monica throughout her life. But he was not her only child. We shall therefore take a brief look at the rest of Monica's family now.

Monica had three children by Patricius, two boys and a girl. The decurion must certainly have been delighted. For a home without children is like a springtime without flowers and birds. Patricius had really married Monica solely to have children. And so when he saw her bending over her children's cradles, one after the other, his happiness induced him to seek to understand and to treat with greater consideration, and finally to follow the guidance of the woman whom Providence had given him as a wife.

Let us take a quick glance at these three children. Augustine became one of the great men of history. It is precisely because of his fame that much less is said about his brother and sister. In fact, they have receded into the shadow of their illustrious brother to the point that very few people even know they lived at all.

The second son of Monica and Patricius was Navigius. He possessed neither the talents nor the torrential passions of his older brother; he experienced neither his excesses nor his repentance. He grew to be a fine man, devout, gentle, intelligent, well-educated, but also timid, retiring, silent, and apparently of frail health. We might say he never left his mother's side. He was to be her comforter when she was saddened by Augustine's errant ways. Navi-

gius married and had a son whom he named Patricius.
It was this nephew of Augustine's who became a
subdeacon at the church of Hippo and to whom the
great doctor alluded in one of his *Sermons*. According
to Augustine's first biographer, Possidius, Navigius
also had two daughters. These nieces of Augustine
would some day take the veil as virgins—the nuns of
that time—in the church under their uncle's care.

Finally, Monica had a daughter about whom we
know even less than Navigius. According to an ancient tradition, she was named Perpetua after one of
the most inspiring martyrs of the early African Church.
She married but was soon widowed. She then went
to live with her brother Augustine, but only until
he was ordained to the priesthood. From that moment
on, according to Possidius, Augustine "refused to
allow any woman to live under the same roof with
him, not even his sister." Augustine declared he was
not rejecting his sister, but all the women who would
come and visit her. It is because of this well-known
reference by Possidius that we know Augustine had
a sister. We also have one of Augustine's letters that
was probably addressed to her. For she became the
superior of a convent of sorts, which Augustine
founded as a complement to his church of Hippo.

Navigius and Perpetua, Augustine's brother and
sister, have been honored in various places among
the ranks of the "Blessed." Thus, Monica brought
forth a whole family of saints.

This is certainly to Monica's credit. She brought
them forth to earthly life, while thinking above all
of obtaining for them the eternal happiness of heaven.
We have not improvised this thought. Augustine himself said it of his mother:

"She brought me forth both in the flesh for this
earthly life and in her heart, in order to bring me
forth to eternal joy."

Understood in this light, motherhood is al-
together sublime. A Christian mother that does not

rise to such heights is not living up to her faith and
to the duties it places upon her. Alas! It is all too
frequent among the mothers of our own time to want
for their children only passing advantages such as
intellectual superiority, chances of "getting ahead"
in the world, and the like, while forgetting at least in
part the true dimensions of the human personality,
those that make it grow to the infinite stature of God
Himself.

The death of Patricius

Before turning to the events that joined the names
of Monica and Augustine for all time, we must complete our account of her role as a wife.

As we have said, Monica was married to Patricius
for eighteen years. It is thought that her husband,
who was 55 years old when he married her, died at
the age of 73 around the year 371. Nothing is known
about his last illness and death. It is certain, however,
that he was converted before he died, that he himself
asked to be baptized, that he received the sacrament
with great fervor and then fell asleep in the Lord.

So Monica had won her husband's soul for heav-
en. Drop by drop, the water had kept falling on the
rock until it had worn it away. Day after day, Patricius
had seen his wife's virtuous conduct. He could not
misjudge her virtues. Now at last the work of grace
was accomplished in him. Monica's persistent prayers
for him were finally answered, as they would be for
Augustine later on.

The holy wife's first victory probably proved a
decisive impetus to obtain the second victory. Now
she knew that baptism had wiped away all her husband's sins, and that she would have the happiness of
seeing him again in heaven. For a soul of faith like
Monica's, this consolation made her forget all the
sufferings and afflictions of her life as Patricius' wife.

But at the time she became a widow, her mother's heart was still deeply troubled. It was through these maternal sufferings that she reached her full spiritual stature before God. In bringing forth her son Augustine to the life of grace she was to win the most enviable of crowns. She would become a saint.

3

The firstborn

Monica
and
Her
Child
Augustine

On the thirteenth of November of the year 354 A.D., Monica gave birth to her first child and named him Augustine. What he would become was hidden in the mystery of human destinies. Could Monica in her humility and modest circumstances even remotely guess that her son would be one of the great men of history, indeed the greatest doctor of the Western Church? Such an idea would have amazed her, to say the least.

The Church, in her admiration for Monica's son Augustine, has not forgotten to be grateful to Monica for the role she played, with God's help, in the growth, the Christian training, and the spiritual awakening of her firstborn.

We say "with God's help" advisedly. Later on, Augustine would see his own coming into the world as God's own doing. We are led to believe that this vision came to him as much through his mother as from his own meditations. Let us therefore cite the passage from the *Confessions* in which Augustine speaks of his birth as ordained by God's own Providence. We shall call this passage *The Sweetness of the Milk,* as does Louis Bertrand in his translation of it.

"Yet, though I am but dust and ashes, suffer me [O Lord!] to utter my plea to Your mercy; suffer me to speak since it is to God's mercy that I speak and not to man's scorn. From You too I might have scorn, but You will return and have compassion on me. What have I to say to You, God, save that I know not where I came from, when I came into this life-in-death — or should I call it death-in-life? I do not know. I only know that the gifts Your mercy had provided sustained me from the first moment: not that I remember it, but so I have heard from the parents of my flesh, the father from whom, and the mother in whom, You fashioned me in time.

"Thus for my sustenance and my delight I had woman's milk: yet it was not my mother or my nurses who stored their breasts for me: it was Yourself, using them to give me the food of my infancy, according to Your ordinance and the riches set by You at every level of creation" *(Confessions,* Book One, VI, pp. 6-7).

Such a philosophy of human life is a far cry from certain forms of modern "existentialism," which claim man just came into being, without knowing where he came from or where he is going. In their view man is just "dropped" onto the earth in a meaningless manner, without any light to guide him, with no law but the law he invents for himself when he reaches adulthood.

For Augustine, as for his loving mother Monica, everything came from God alone — the parents who beget and bring forth, the sweet milk that nurtures, the capacities for growth that progressively form the man of tomorrow.

In the same passage of his *Confessions,* Augustine goes on to speak of Monica's joys as a young mother:

"All good things are from You, O God, and *from God is all my health.* But this I have learned since: You have made it abundantly clear by all that I have seen You give, within me and about me. For at that time I knew how to suck, to lie quiet when I was content, to cry when I was in pain: and that was all I knew" (*Confessions,* Book One, VI, p. 7).

That is what early infancy is like. But soon Monica experienced an intense emotion she would always remember, and that she was to talk about with her son later: his first smile! Augustine continues:

"Later I added smiling to the things I could do, first in sleep, then awake. This again I have on the word of others, for naturally I do not remember; in any event, I believe it, for I have seen other infants do the same" *(Ibid.).*

And then the first sparks of intelligence appeared! The happy mother, eagerly watching her son's development, could not fail to see it.

"And gradually I began to notice where I was, and the will grew in me to make my wants known to those who might satisfy them; but I could not, for my wants were within me and those others were outside: nor had they any faculty enabling them to enter into my mind. So I would fling my arms and legs about and utter sounds, making the few gestures in my power—these being as apt to express my wishes as I could make them: but they were not very apt. And when I did not get what I wanted, either because my wishes were not clear or the things not good for me, I was in a rage—with my parents as though I had a right to their submission, with free human beings as though they had been bound to serve me; and I took my revenge in screams" *(Ibid.).*

Early training

After the weeks and months of early infancy, Augustine's "education" began. By this we mean the long succession of efforts to develop the child's faculties and his interior awareness. Perhaps we should say that Monica had begun his education much sooner, by her countless prayers. St. Francis de Sales, in his *Introduction to the Devout Life,* has written: "When St. Monica was pregnant with the great St. Augustine, she dedicated him, through several offerings, to the Christian religion and to the service of God's glory, as he himself has testified, saying that he had already tasted the salt of God within his mother's womb."

As soon as Augustine was born he had been carried to the church, not to be baptized — for that required a rather long preparation — but to be registered as a catechumen through rites preparatory for baptism. Although he was not yet baptized, he was at least an aspirant for the sacrament of regeneration. He was included among the members of the Church, he had received the sign of the cross on his forehead. The symbolic salt had been placed on his lips. Augustine's religious education in the strict sense began when he was old enough to understand what his mother was saying to him, to join his hands and lisp after her the ineffable name of Jesus. We can picture this intelligent little boy paying close attention to his mother as she tried to tell him in simple words what the meaning of life was, make him understand the great truth that he would later express in his own words:

"You have made us for Yourself, O God, and our hearts are restless until they rest in You!"

Yes, we are made for God, and that is our immense greatness! Monica was always talking to Augustine about God's love for us, about the gifts He never tires of lavishing upon us, about the crib of

Bethlehem, the sweet Virgin Mary, the shepherds, the
cave where she brought Him forth, and the visit of
the Wise Men. It was a divine story, and yet so well
adapted to human understanding. And how it touches
the heart of a child when told by a beloved mother.
Monica thus laid foundations in the child's heart
that would be the strength of his whole life.

It is Augustine who tells us that Monica did all
these things:

"Even as a boy, of course, I had heard of an eternal life promised because the Lord our God had come
down in His humility upon our pride" (*Confessions*,
Book One, XI, p. 14).

Who can doubt that Monica was the one who
taught Augustine these truths, since his father was
still a pagan and far removed from these sublime
teachings?

In another passage of his *Confessions*, Augustine
declares that when as a young man he opened a book
and failed to find the name of Jesus Christ in it he
found no pleasure in it.

It was during this time that Monica told her son
the accounts of her own youth in order to train him
in Christian living, including the close call she had
had with the vice of alcoholism. Obviously, she was
not afraid to confess her weaknesses, if she could
thereby preserve the integrity of her son's conscience.
This did not save him from falling into the corrupt
practices of the world. But even in his waywardness,
he always had a deep nostalgia for beauty, a need for
God, a thirst for greatness. Later on, through the intercession of his mother's tears, divine grace would re-
awaken all these noble inclinations and powerfully
rekindle them.

A moment of danger

A passage in the *Confessions* shows how deeply
Monica's teaching had impressed her son. The in-

cident occurred when he was nine or ten years old, around 363 or 364 A.D.

"When I was still a child, I fell gravely ill with some abdominal trouble and was close to death. You saw, Lord—for You were even then guarding me—with what earnest faith I besought the piety of my own mother, and of the Church which is the mother of us all, that I might receive the baptism of Your Christ, my Lord and my God" (Confessions, Book One, XI, p. 14).

Let us reflect on the child's insistence. He must already have had a wonderful understanding of life's meaning to think only of eternity in the face of death. Are there many children in our own day who would take upon themselves to beg for the last sacraments when in peril of death? Obviously Monica had not wasted her time training her son. Augustine witnesses to it in concluding the account:

"The mother of my flesh was in heavy anxiety, since with a heart chaste in Your faith she was ever in deep travail for my eternal salvation, and would have proceeded without delay to have me consecrated and washed clean by the sacrament of salvation, while I confessed You, Lord Jesus, unto the remission of sins..." (Ibid.).

However, this was only an alert. As everyone scurried around the dying child, suddenly his choking and gasps stopped. All danger seemed over. There was no longer any thought of baptizing him at that time. The thinking on the matter was that a child faced so many worldly temptations to which he would almost surely yield that it was better for him to be a simple catechumen than a baptized Christian whose sins would be more serious. Augustine, along with all the Church Fathers of his time, would later combat this idea as erroneous, and helped to eradicate it from the Church. However when he was a child, this custom was still so deeply rooted that we can understand why Monica did not have her son baptized even though there was an excellent opportunity for doing so.

Early studies

While Augustine very early revealed signs of great intellect, no one could yet foresee to what heights he would rise. Like all other children of respectable families, he was sent to school. His earliest record as a scholar was disappointing. At first he gave evidence of what looked like invincible laziness and a deplorable dislike for study, as he himself has admitted. When he wrote his *Confessions* at the age of 46 or so, he still remembered the time when he had to mechanically mumble the letters of the alphabet and repeat in sing-song fashion with the others: 1 + 1 make 2; 2 + 2 make 4! His mother naturally knew about his restiveness, and sought to console and encourage him. She would alternate promises with threats and punishments. Hasn't every mother gone through such episodes? As for Augustine, he later admitted he sought to get around the demands made upon him by his father, his mother and his teachers by means of evasions and even lies.

However, he did not lack adult advice. His mother prevailed upon some older persons to exhort him. They spoke to him about the need of learning. They told him God was invisible and helps us when we learn how to pray to Him. His mother had been telling him these things for a long time. But Augustine says he prayed above all that he would not be beaten at school. And his prayers were not answered. And then everyone made fun of him and his prayers: "...my elders and even my parents, who certainly wished me no harm, treated my stripes as a huge joke, which they were far from being to me" (*Confessions*, Book One, IX, p. 12).

Obviously Monica had a "difficult" child. No matter how much she commanded and encouraged, chided and scolded, he still liked play better than study. And he was not very obedient. Yet he was certainly not lacking in talent. He learned easily and remembered everything he learned. But he had to be forced to study. And so Monica forced him, for his own good, but not without considerable suffering on her own part.

Pagan studies

A still more serious danger threatened Augustine when he finally threw himself with enthusiasm into more advanced studies.

He was no longer satisfied with the school of Tagaste. His father was now proud of his attainments and wanted to "push him ahead" out of ambition for his future. This meant he had to be entrusted to better teachers, to a more advanced school. There was a little town called Madaura a few miles from Tagaste, famous for its schools of rhetoric and literature. Augustine's parents decided to send him there.

It must have been a great sacrifice for Monica to be separated from her son. He was to return home only at vacation time. But, she thought, it was for his good, and so she did not hesitate. She apparently did not suspect the moral peril her child would encounter there, in spite of everything she had done to protect him up to that time. He was probably thirteen or fourteen years old, the age when the passions awaken. He was to find himself in an almost completely pagan milieu, under the guidance of pagan teachers. He would be expected to follow the course of study of the time, which consisted in reading the Greek and Roman classics.

The custom was for the teacher to read aloud texts from masterpieces of Greek and Latin literature, explaining their beauties. Actually, this method of delving into a text and bringing out its nuances of meaning was excellent. Later, Augustine wisely used it in his study of the sacred books of Scripture.

But let us come back to him at the age of fifteen. By this time he had developed a passionate interest in reading. Gone now was his eagerness for games. He read voraciously the works of Homer, Virgil, Cicero, and Ovid. The emotions described in these works set him afire. For some reason he seems to have had an aversion for Greek, which he would never completely overcome. But Virgil aroused his enthusiasm. Although he didn't realize it, what fascinated him about Virgil was the way he presented the most violent aspects of human love. He later said that he could not read the account of Dido's ill-fated love for Aeneas without weeping. When he was forbidden to spend so much time in such reading, he wept until the books were returned to him. And then he would weep as he read them again, drinking in the passions that were so vividly portrayed by the pagan poets. To quote his own words: "My one desire in those days was to love and be loved."

But Augustine was not satisfied to remain within the bounds of sweet friendship. He soon began to burn with evil desires. He himself has acknowledged it:

"Arrived now at adolescence I burned for all the satisfactions of hell, and I sank to the animal in a succession of dark lusts: *my beauty consumed away,* and I stank in Your eyes, yet was pleasing in my own and anxious to please the eyes of men" (*Confessions,* Book Two, I, p. 27).

Be it said that Augustine still maintained external propriety. His turmoil was within. His mother may have been worried, but thought: "There's nothing serious yet!" For Augustine gave more and more evidence of extraordinary aptitudes. He had many successes at Madaura. He stood out among his fellow students, and his teachers promised him a great future. Patricius was so delighted with the compliments he heard about his son that he decided to send him to Carthage, Africa's greatest city, so that he might attend schools of greater renown and prove his abilities. This involved very great expense for the family, but Patricius did not hesitate. As he did not have the funds necessary to carry out his plans, he brought Augustine back to Tagaste for a year. Meanwhile, he hoped to set aside the money he would need to provide for his son's advanced studies.

Monica was all in favor of these high ambitions. Later on Augustine would suggest that she had perhaps lacked in prudence, that she had not sufficiently gauged the terrible dangers that would threaten her firstborn son's soul. But after all, she was still completely unaware of the temptations that were assailing him. She was like so many other mothers who cannot bring themselves to realize that their offspring have emerged from the cocoon of childhood. She must have rejoiced even more than his father over his successes. When she saw how studious he was, how greatly admired, how eloquent, she imagined he was still perfectly innocent and incapable of falling into sin.

For his part, as he would later reveal in his *Confessions,* Augustine did his best to hide from his mother what was going on in his soul. During the year he lived at home with his parents—probably from 369 to 370—he kept from her his deep inner turmoil. She didn't notice anything, she didn't know anything. And yet an increasingly violent drama was unfolding:

"But during that sixteenth year from Madaura and Carthage, owing to the narrowness of the family fortunes I did not go to school, but lived idly at home with my parents. The briars of unclean lusts grew so that they towered over my head, and there was no hand to root them out" (*Confessions,* Book Two, III, p. 29).

And the same thing happened to him that implacably happens to all who violate the order established by divine Wisdom. As soon as we violate God's order, it retaliates. Evil becomes contagious within the sinner. A punishment flows from the sin itself that is in a sense immanent to the sin. St. Augustine was to understand this very well in later years:

"Your wrath had grown mighty against me and I knew it not. I had grown deaf from the clanging of the chain of my mortality, the punishment for the pride of my soul: and I departed further from You, and I was tossed about and wasted and poured out and boiling over in my fornications: and You were silent, O my late-won Joy. You were silent, and I, arrogant and depressed, weary and restless, wandered further and further from You into more and more sins which could bear no fruit save sorrows" (*Confessions*, Book Two, II, pp. 27-28).

In such a state, how could Augustine be happy? And yet this was a favor from God. Augustine didn't realize it, but his failure to find happiness in vice was a great blessing. His mother's early training continued to protect him against the most obdurate hardness of heart. Besides, we can be sure that although Monica didn't know how low her son had fallen, she was constantly praying for him and for his future. In later years, Augustine reminisced:

"You [O Lord] were always by me, mercifully hard upon me, and besprinkling all my illicit pleasures with certain elements of bitterness, to draw me on to seek for pleasures in which no bitterness should be" (*ibid.*).

Strangely enough, Augustine turned to God in prayer at least once in a while, inspired by his mother's example. Outwardly he maintained decorum by continuing to go to church as he had done as a child. It was there that he sometimes cried out to his God. He even went so far as to beg God to help him practice the virtue of purity, which his mother urged upon him. But he had a rather odd way of praying, as he himself has told us:

"During my most shameful adolescence, nay, at the very start of this adolescence, I used to ask You (O my God) for chastity, and I used to say to You: 'Grant me chastity and continence, but not yet!' I feared my plea would be too quickly answered and I would be too soon healed of this sickness of concupiscence, for I preferred to satisfy it than to see it extinguished!"

Did such a prayer deserve an answer? It may have left the way open for hope in the future. But for the time being the young man's moral condition continued to worsen. He came to enjoy only evil company, to desire evil for its own sake, and to commit absurd acts, simply to amuse himself by living a disorderly life. We can judge his moral outlook for ourselves from his *Confessions:*

"Your law, O Lord, punishes theft; and this law is so written in the hearts of men that not even the breaking of it blots it out: for no thief bears calmly being stolen from—not even if he is rich and the other steals through want. Yet I chose to steal, and not because want drove me to it—unless a want of justice and contempt for it and an excess for iniquity. For I stole things which I already had in plenty and of better quality. Nor had I any desire to enjoy the things I stole, but only the stealing of them and the sin.

"There was a pear tree near our vineyard, heavy with fruit, but fruit that was not particularly tempting either to look at or to taste. A group of young blackguards, and I among them, went out to knock down the pears and carry them off late one night, for it was our bad habit to carry on our games in the streets till very late. We carried off an immense load of pears, not to eat—for we barely tasted them before throwing them to the hogs. Our only pleasure in doing it was that it was forbidden" (Book Two, IV, pp. 31-32).

Augustine had indeed sunk very low, and he was only sixteen years old. Monica was beginning to realize what was happening to him, although she had as yet no idea how far her son's soul had been ravaged by sin. Still greater trials were in store for her, as we shall relate later.

We shall close this chapter by talking briefly about Monica's relations with her husband's mother.

Monica and her mother-in-law

Here again, whatever we know comes to us from Augustine. And from what he tells us of his paternal grandmother, she was a rather imperious lady who made life hard for her daughter-in-law, at least in the beginning. What was even more serious was that the mother-in-law was suspicious and haughty, and kept questioning the slaves of the household about Monica. To win her favor, they used to say all sorts of evil things about the young wife. As a result, relations between the two women became increasingly tense. But Monica, who showed such patience toward her husband, was equally patient with her mother-in-law. She endured all affronts without anger or rancor. In the end she overcame the prejudices of the woman who was persecuting her.

Actually, Patricius' mother was honest and well-meaning. She finally came to realize that the household slaves had been lying to her out of false loyalty. So she decided to put an end to their intrigues. A few inquiries on her part soon proved that the stories they had told her about Monica were all lies. Without saying a word to Monica about it, she went directly to her son. And Patricius, who was a stern master, had the servants whipped.

After this sharp reprimand, Monica's mother-in-law declared that if any of the women servants came to her carrying tales about her daughter-in-law, thinking they were pleasing her, they would be punished again in the same way. Understandably, this put an end to the persecution. From that moment on, Monica lived with her mother-in-law in an atmosphere of great affection and mutual trust.

4

The Great Trials

A mother's fears

Patricius was the first to notice that his son had reached sexual maturity. At the time he was already a catechumen, and well on the way to becoming a Christian. When he noticed his son was troubled by the carnal passions he himself had experienced so powerfully, he did not at first feel any great anxiety for Augustine's spiritual welfare. Rather, he began to think of marrying him off. We read in the *Confessions* that Patricius was actually delighted to discover his son had become a man, "because he could already see himself becoming a grandfather."

Monica looked at things very differently. To quote Augustine:

"But in my mother's breast You had already laid the foundation of Your temple and begun Your holy habitation: whereas my father was still only a catechumen, and a new catechumen at that. So that she was stricken with a holy fear. And though I was not as yet baptized, she was in terror of my walking in the crooked ways of those who walk with their backs towards You and not their faces" (*Confessions*, Book Two, III, p. 30).

Monica was not content to lament and weep. She wanted to accomplish her duty as a mother to the fullest extent possible. Taking her son aside, she tried to get him to confide in her. She spoke to him with all the tenderness at her command. She warned him against passions whose burgeoning she surmised within him, without knowing how far they already consumed him. She spoke to him frankly of his obligations, pointing out potential dangers to a stable and happy marriage.

Augustine let his mother talk, but said nothing. Her words just slid over his mind and heart. He considered everything she said to be just "woman talk," which he, as a young man, would have been ashamed to take seriously. In his adolescent pride and intensity, he refused to let himself be "bossed around" by a woman, even his own mother. Later, he confessed: "You were speaking to me through her [my God!], and in ignoring her I was ignoring You!" (*Confessions*, Book Two, III, p. 30)

Monica saw she was not winning her fight for her son's soul. She realized that while Augustine did not contradict her, he had no intention of following her wise counsel. Instead, he began to avoid her, to evade any intimate conversations with her. She could not fail to understand there was a regrettable estrangement between them. This was the beginning of a period of great trials for her.

Carthage

Patricius' plans were proceeding according to schedule. It had been decided once and for all that

Augustine would go to Carthage to engage in more advanced study as soon as the family budget permitted.

A year's delay had been conceded. Monica saw the moment of her son's departure approach with secret terror, but without being able to oppose it. She may have thought her son's concern for his future would have an effect on his behavior, and that it was better for him to be removed from his indolent life at Tagaste, or perhaps that there was no real remedy to his spiritual troubles other than prayer.

So Monica resolved to redouble her entreaties before God, to preserve her son by her tears, when distance prevented her from protecting him by her presence, her glances, and her counsels. In any event, there was no change in plans for Augustine. Patricius had made up his mind to that, and Monica could only bow to her husband's wishes.

Augustine left for Carthage, probably in the fall of the year 370. He was then just about sixteen, as his birthday was in November.

Carthage was then like another Rome, one of the most brilliant centers of Roman civilization, a city that displayed great luxury, a city of pleasures, to which flocked students from the entire Roman province of Africa, more eager for freedom and even licentiousness, than for human knowledge. The boldest of these students had assumed or been given a nickname of which they were proud. They were called the *Eversores*, that is to say, the *Overturners* or *Ravagers*.

Augustine, although inwardly consumed with passion, was outwardly timid and reserved. But instead of being glad he was not as vulgar and violent as his companions, he suffered from a kind of inferiority complex in their presence. He refers to this feeling as a "shame of the sense of shame that kept me from being like them" *(Confessions*, Book Three, III, p. 44). Only one thing redeemed him in his own eyes, and this was his success in his studies. To quote his own words:

"By this time I was a leader in the School of Rhetoric and I enjoyed this high station and was arrogant and swollen with importance: You know, O Lord, that I was far quieter in my behavior and had no share in the riotousness.... I was with them and I did for the most part enjoy their companionship, though I abominated the acts that were their specialty —as when they made a butt of some hapless newcomer, assailing him with really cruel mockery for no reason whatever..." (*Confessions*, Book Three, III, p. 44).

He was obsessed with only one thing, as he tells us:

"I was not yet in love, but I was in love with love, and from the very depth of my need...I sought some object to love, since I was in love with loving.... For within I was hungry, all for want of that spiritual food which is Yourself, my God; yet [though I was hungry for want of it] I did not hunger for it: I had no desire whatever for incorruptible food, not because I had it in abundance but the emptier I was, the more I hated the thought of it. Because of all this my soul was sick, and broke out in sores, whose itch I agonized to scratch with the rub of carnal things.... My longing then was to love and to be loved..." (*Confessions*, Book Three, I, p. 41).

He could not fail to find one day or other what he was seeking so avidly. He sought it in the theater. He says: "I developed a passion for stage plays, with the mirror they held up to my own miseries and the fuel they poured on my flame" (*Confessions*, Book Three, II, pp. 41-42).

But when the play was over he would go out, more eager than ever to find an occasion to sin. He continued to attend Church services, but even there he found no peace because he really didn't want

peace any more. He has related one such incident as
follows:

"For I dared so far one day within the walls of
Your church and during the very celebration of Your
mysteries to desire and carry out an act worthy of the
fruits of death. For this You lashed me with the
heaviest punishments, yet the punishments were as
nothing to the guilt of my act. O my God, my ex-
ceeding great Mercy, my Refuge from the fierce
dangers among which I wandered in my arrogance,
going ever further from You, loving my way and not
Your ways, in love with my runaway liberty" (Confessions, Book Three, III, p. 44).

Finally, he did have the love affair he had
yearned so much for. He does not mention in his
Confessions the name of the woman, or rather the
young girl, who became his companion without
benefit of marriage.

But he was no happier now than before, as he
himself later avowed:

"And I did fall in love, simply from wanting to.
O my God, my Mercy, with how much bitterness did
You in Your goodness sprinkle the delights of that
time! I was loved, and our love came to the bond of
consummation: I wore my chains with bliss but with
torment too, for I was scourged with the red hot rods
of jealousy, with suspicions and fears and tempers
and quarrels" (Confessions, Book Three, I, p. 41).

It should however be pointed out that both
Augustine and his companion were faithful to each
other, even if their relationship was sinful and illicit.
This young woman was to remain with him for fifteen
years. She finally left him amid many tears only at
the moment of his conversion. She, too, was converted
after her lover's example. It is thought she withdrew
to a convent to belong to God alone the remaining
days of her life.

So we see that Augustine was not a completely
dissolute and flighty person. He was capable of

enduring love. Everything tends to indicate that Augustine's first liaison was what novels might call "a great and fated love." But from what he himself tells us, and probably precisely because it was so passionate, this love was a very stormy one. Was he the jealous party? Or was it she? Or rather, were they not both jealous? We do not know for certain, but at any rate there were frequent scenes, recriminations, angry outbursts, tears, and then reconciliations. This we can glean from the *Confessions*.

As early as 372, when Augustine was only eighteen years old, he became a father. In the first rapture of his joy, he dared to call his son *Adeodatus*, which means *"God-given."* In later years after the death of this beloved son for whom there were such high hopes, he dared call him only *"the son of my sin."* Looking back, this portion of his life seemed like a nightmare. "That was my life," he wrote. "O my God, was it really a life?"

A mother's tears

Although Augustine had been able to conceal his dissolute life from his mother up to that time, he was now forced to let her know his situation. This urgency was increased by his pressing financial problems. His father had died, leaving only a modest estate. He had depleted his resources to defray the heavy expense of his sons' studies. Now that Monica was a widow, she was resolved to assume even the most rigorous sacrifices to help her beloved son prepare for what promised to be a brilliant future. But precisely because of her generosity, Augustine felt obliged to lay bare to her the details of his new situation, which involved the support of an illegitimate wife and son.

We can imagine Monica's dismay when she learned what had been going on in Carthage. Any

mother can understand her tears. For many years
to come she was to live a life of grueling sorrow. Year
after year she wept. But she wept before God in perfect obedience and resignation, while begging His
help. Indeed, Monica's tears were prayers, prayers
that finally obtained the conversion of a straying son.

In a sense we can say Christian tradition has
canonized Monica's tears. The Church recalls them in
the prayers for the feast of St. Monica. In the Mass
dedicated to her memory, the Gospel is taken from
St. Luke and calls to mind how Jesus raised from the
dead the only son of the widow of Naim. For Monica's
tears were beseeching from God's mercy the resur-
rection of a soul on the road to perdition, and yet
such a beloved and great soul! In the ancient Roman
Office of St. Monica, all the antiphons alluded to
her tears. We offer a modern translation of them:

"*Antiphon 1*. This mother wept and prayed
diligently so as to obtain the conversion of her son
Augustine."

"*Antiphon 2*. O blessed and happy mother,
who were one day to have your prayers answered
according to the vastness of your desires! Meanwhile, this afflicted mother wept day and night,
praying fervently for her son."

"*Antiphon 3*. Behold, behold, this widow who
knows how to weep! She constantly shed bitter tears
for her son!"

"*Antiphon 4*. The rivers of tears that fell from
this holy mother's eyes have raised their voices,
Lord, they have raised their voices."

"*Antiphon 5*. This inconsolable mother wept
tears beyond counting...."

In the light of these antiphons, the feast of
St. Monica has been called by some "the feast of a
mother's tears."

An unexpected benefactor

Touching as Monica's tears may seem to us now, they could not solve the heavy problems she faced. She had two other children, for whom she had to provide as well as her eldest son. Where could she find the necessary financial resources, especially if Augustine, who was still far from being able to earn his own living, was to pursue his studies as she so earnestly desired?

Under the circumstances, her tears seem to have obtained an initial response. God would in His own good time grant the conversion of her son, for whom He had such lofty plans. In the meantime, He inspired a rich resident of Tagaste, no doubt a friend of Patricius, to come to the aid of this unfortunate family.

Augustine's resounding successes at Madaura, the accounts of him already coming out of Carthage, and the high hopes Patricius had held for him, all must have made an impression on the little town. A man named Romanianus decided he would be performing a worthy action by offering the mother and son the help they needed so badly. Augustine himself has recounted it in one of his writings. This townsman was very rich. Better still, he had a generous heart and sensed Augustine's genius. He opened his purse, but with all the tact and graciousness the situation demanded, so as not to offend such a noble and cultivated mother. His proffered aid was liberal enough to allow Monica to go and live in Carthage, so she could keep a closer watch on her eldest son. If we read Augustine's words carefully, it would appear that Romanianus' largesses had begun during Patricius' lifetime and were merely increased after his death in 371.

The passage to which we refer is not from the *Confessions* but from a work entitled *Contra academicos* ("Against the Academics") which we might translate today as: *Against the Agnostics* or *Against the Sceptics*, that is to say, against those who doubt everything. Augustine writes:

"O Romanianus, shall I never be able to thank you? Was it not you who, at the time when I, a poor young man, was planning to pursue my studies in a distant city, offered me your house, your purse, and what is far more, your very heart? And when I suffered the loss of my father, was it not you who consoled me with your friendship, sustained me with your counsels, and helped me with your fortune? Yes, in Tagaste, our little town, you cast a beginning of glory upon me, by honoring me publicly with your friendship and offering me half of your house."

This passage throws light on the means that made it possible for Monica to live close to her son. She found a way of showing her gratitude to Romanianus by taking care of his son Licentius in Carthage, surrounding him with her love and serving as a foster-mother to him just as Romanianus was a kind of foster-father to Augustine.

And so Monica came to live in the big city. There she continued to pray and weep, but her primary concern was to encourage Augustine in his studies. We know from him that she realized how important they were. In his *Confessions* he tells us that although his father pushed him to study out of worldly ambition, Monica for her part looked upon his studies as a means of bringing him back to his God. With astonishing intuition, this mother understood that although "a little knowledge turns one away from God, much knowledge brings one back to Him."

In any case, Monica's tearful prayers won an initial skirmish when her son Augustine, with his great gift for higher philosophy, came upon a book that opened up new horizons for him. This book was Cicero's *Hortensius*.

Augustine reads Hortensius

Hortensius was a Roman orator, a few years older than Cicero and the latter's rival in the field of rhetoric. Cicero's book about him has been lost. But we know from Augustine the lessons he learned from it. It was in the year 373. Augustine tells us he was then nineteen years old, and his father had been dead two years.

In his book, Cicero set forth the various systems of philosophy then held in honor by the Graeco-Roman world. Above all, he gave highest praise to philosophy per se. He refuted the vain subtleties of the Sophists and returned to the loftier traditions of Socrates and Plato. Augustine was entranced and even transformed. He had only been looking for generally admired literary forms in Cicero's works. And now, underneath the words he was discovering profound and noble thought. He might have said: "I was looking for an author, and I found a man!"

Augustine realized that while everyone raved over Cicero's language, few were competent to appreciate his taste for flights of the spirit. Augustine understood that *Hortensius* was primarily an exhortation to the study of philosophy.

"Quite definitely it changed the direction of my mind, altered my prayers to You, O Lord, and gave me a new purpose and ambition. Suddenly all the vanity I had hoped in I saw as worthless, and with an incredible intensity of desire I longed after immortal wisdom. I had begun that journey upwards by which I was to return to You. ...I...was receiving money from my mother for the continuance of my study of eloquence. But I used that book not for the sharpening of my tongue; what won me in it was what it said, not the excellence of its phrasing" (*Confessions*, Book Three, IV, p. 45).

What was the message of *Hortensius* as Augustine understood it? He read the book with all the insights his Christian education had provided him. Without being distinctly aware of it, he went farther than Cicero because deep in his soul lived the teachings of Christ.

"How did I then burn, my God, how did I burn to wing upwards from earthly delights to You. But I had no notion what You were to do with me. For with You is wisdom. Now love of wisdom is what is meant by the Greek word philosophy, and it was to philosophy that that book set me so ardently" *(ibid.)*.

At that period of his life Augustine probably did not make a clear distinction between profane philosophy and the teachings of Christian wisdom. He was not yet acquainted with the writings of St. Paul on which he would later meditate with such enthusiasm. But, as he himself admitted, it was already a very important step toward God to become enamored of human wisdom and to find that Cicero was exhorting him in that direction.

Nevertheless, something was lacking in Augustine's reading. It was on this point that the remembrance of his mother's teachings proved most helpful. To use his own words:

"The book excited and inflamed me; in my ardor the only thing I found lacking was that *the name of Christ was not there!* For with my mother's milk my infant heart had drunk in, and still held deep down in it, that name according to Your mercy, O Lord, the name of Your Son, my Savior; and whatever lacked that name, no matter how learned and excellently written and true, *could not win me wholly*" *(op. cit.,* p. 46).

Given Augustine's passionate temperament, we can imagine he eagerly shared his intellectual discoveries with his mother, discussing with her the books he read and the great ideas that were stirring in his mind. Were Monica's persistent prayers for her son's conversion about to be answered?

Augustine reads the Scriptures

Monica may have thought the great moment had finally come when her young philosopher-son asked to read the Scripture scrolls. If a mere man like Cicero could excite him to such a degree, what, then, of God's own word! Sad to say, the reading of Scripture did not produce the effect Monica so earnestly hoped.

In any event, Augustine began to read the Bible. It would help us to know where he began. A study of the Gospels and the epistles of St. Paul might have conquered him. However at that period of his life he was still chiefly concerned with matters of rhetoric. He could discern the truth only when couched in beautiful language. And we cannot deny that the Scriptures do not impress us primarily by their elegant style. To read them fruitfully, one must approach them in a spirit of humble faith. Augustine has testified to this:

"So I resolved to make some study of the Sacred Scriptures and find what kind of books they were. But what I came upon was something not grasped by the proud, not revealed either to children, something utterly humble in the hearing but sublime in the doing, and shrouded deep in mystery. And I was not of the nature to enter into it or bend my neck to follow it. When I first read those Scriptures, I did not feel in the least what I have just said; they seemed to me unworthy to be compared with the majesty of Cicero. My conceit was repelled by their simplicity, and I had not the mind to penetrate into their depths. They were indeed of a nature to grow in Your little ones. But I could not bear to be a little one; I was only swollen with pride, but to myself I seemed a very big man" (*Confessions*, Book Three, V, p. 46).

In one of his sermons to his flock in Hippo, Augustine later said:

"Learn from my experience. When I was a young man I tried to read the Sacred Scriptures, but my sinful life closed my mind to what they were saying. Since my heart was not pure, I could not penetrate their meaning."

So we see that at eighteen Augustine still had a long way to go. We can well wonder whether the circumstances of his personal life did not cruelly impede his spiritual progress. Otherwise the perfect light of the Christian faith might have been revealed to his eyes at that time. Nevertheless, the lessons *Hortensius* taught him were not lost. Nothing was wasted of the riches of goodness that God had bestowed on him through His grace or through his mother's teaching and prayers.

As for Monica, she continued to pray for her son, and would not let anything discourage her. In the end, she was sure Augustine would come to understand. But that would take twelve more years!

5

Monica Perseveres

Manichaeism

Monica had nurtured high hopes. Her son's reading of *Hortensius* had snatched him away from earthly concerns and kindled great desires for wisdom in his soul. But he could not conceive of wisdom without the name of Christ. So he had been impelled to seek this divine name in the Scriptures.

Augustine's innate pride kept him from returning directly to the faith of his childhood. Besides, Providence, in its secret workings, refused to reveal itself to him until he was purified. And so he continued to grope, to reach out in the darkness that enveloped him. In his search he embraced the grossest errors, those of the Manichaeans and remained enslaved to them for nine whole years.

Monica would have to pray and weep still longer. But amid all these trials her own faith never wavered. She could easily have been conquered by Augustine's budding genius, the ease with which he grasped the loftiest philosophical doctrines, and his eloquence. And then she might have followed him blindly into error. For a mother without much education and lacking character can easily be dazzled by the talents and words of a son far above her intellectually.

In Monica's case, the temptation to follow her son's thinking was all the stronger because of their frequent and lively discussions of these matters. Would he come back to her or would she lean in his direction?

The question never arose in the mind of this holy mother. She always knew without the shadow of a doubt that hers was the one true, legitimate, and saving faith.

What happened to Augustine during those nine years? Instead of continuing to attend church with his mother he strayed into the false and dangerous sect of the Manichaeans.

Without going into details about the doctrines of this sect which later disappeared, suffice it to say that it was named for a certain Manes, born in ancient Babylon around the year 216 A.D. and who died around 276 A.D.

The Manichaean doctrine, which was to be revived in thirteenth-century France as Albigensianism, was based on a dualistic view of good and evil. According to Manes, from all eternity there have been two principles, Good and Evil. In short, Satan is no less eternal than God, and he is God's rival, His imitator, almost His equal. It is not surprising, therefore, that our world is divided as between good and evil. Far more serious, our very nature is the battlefield between good and evil, between God and Satan. We are not responsible for this conflict within us, and we are powerless to control it.

Manes did not completely reject the name of Christ, without which Augustine found no charm in the world. But in his view Christ was only one of God's heralds. Indeed, Christ Himself had been obliged to fight Satan. When the Gospel was read in the spirit of Manes, it seemed to witness to this dualism.

A man like Augustine could readily be tempted to claim that he was not really responsible for his immoral actions. He could say he had been the hapless victim of evil, and hence had no need to torment himself about his past. Manichaeism gave him to think that salvation consisted in faith alone, without works. This doctrine was to resurface centuries later in the teachings of Martin Luther, although in another form. Perhaps it would be more exact to say that for the Manichaeans the accomplishment of one good work sufficed, as we shall relate later on. This one work that assured salvation was to provide for the needs of the elect or saints of the sect.

Besides, Manichaeism was a secret society. Its members held their assemblies in hiding. This must have been an added charm to Augustine's way of thinking. For gnawed by remorse for his past misdeeds, he must have been attracted to a doctrine that offered such plausible excuses. Manichaeism was then practiced by a number of the leading citizens of Carthage, including some who had the gift of elegant and flowing speech which Augustine prized so highly.

The Manichaeans openly declared among themselves that they wanted to appeal only to human reason and proposed only teachings that were easy to understand. They repudiated what they called the harsh and stern authority of the Church, and claimed, in the final analysis, one could believe whatever one pleased in the Manichaean Church. Granted, the Manichaeans used many expressions that could be misunderstood. They were always talking about Jesus Christ and the Holy Spirit, the way the Catholics did. To quote Augustine: "These words were always on their lips, but when they spoke them they were only meaningless sounds, and their hearts were empty of their true sense."

"Truth! Truth!" This was the Manichaeans' constant cry. And it was truth that young Augustine was so earnestly seeking.

We can easily picture Augustine in those days, completely engrossed with the new ideas he was discovering, and expounding them in his conversations at home. Monica, for her part, was hard-pressed to defend her convictions against her son's Manichaean views.

Monica's attitude

Augustine's *Confessions* tell us how Monica responded to the Manichaean fabrications her son brazenly propounded before her and the rest of the family. Addressing himself to God, as he does throughout this beautiful book, he writes:

"And You sent Your hand from above, and raised my soul out of that depth of darkness, because my mother, Your faithful one, wept to You for me more bitterly than mothers weep for the bodily deaths of their children. For by the faith and the spirit which she had from You, she saw me as dead; and You heard her, Lord. You heard her and did not despise her tears when they flowed down and watered the earth against which she pressed her face wherever she prayed. You heard her" (*Confessions*, Book Three, XI, p. 55).

On the same page of his *Confessions* Augustine tells us about an incident that occurred between him and his mother. Monica finally became indignant

over the blasphemies that came pouring out of
Augustine's mouth. For, with the Manichaeans he
was constantly scoffing at the patriarchs and prophets
of the Old Testament whom the Catholic Church
holds in such high esteem. She declared she could
no longer sit down at table with a son who uttered
such nonsense. She therefore decided to leave her
home and live elsewhere. However she planned not
to go so far that she could not be available to help
her beloved son if the opportunity arose. Before
she could execute her intention she had a warning
dream that made her change her mind. Here is how
Augustine tells about it:

"In her dream she saw herself standing on a
wooden rule and a youth all radiant coming to her
cheerful and smiling upon her, whereas she was
grieving and heavy with her grief. He asked her — not
to learn from her but, as is the way of visions, to
teach her — the causes of her sorrow and the tears
she daily shed. She replied that she was mourning
for the loss of my soul. He commanded her to be at
peace and told her to observe carefully and she
would see that where she was, there was I also.
She looked, and saw me standing alongside her on
the same rule" (*Confessions*, Book Three, XI, p. 55).

Monica took the dream to be a happy portent from
heaven. Like a true African woman, she believed in
dreams when they appeared to have a clearly defin-
able meaning. She understood the vision to be a
sign that her prayers would be answered. Some day
her son would be at her side, on the same rule —
adhering to the same rule of faith! Of this she had
no doubt. So she returned to Augustine's side. In the
dream she had been commanded to stop weeping.
She still could not always restrain her tears, but now
her weeping was tempered with hope.

The mother decided to tell her son about the
dream that had brought her so much consolation.
He himself agreed that it must have come from God.

In the beginning, though, he tried to quibble. He has related the episode as follows:

"...when she had told me her vision and I tried to interpret it to mean that she must not despair of one day being as I was, she answered without an instant's hesitation: 'No. For it was not said to me where he is, you are, but where you are, he is.' I confess to You, O Lord, that if I remember aright — and I have often spoken of it since — I was more deeply moved by that answer which You gave through my mother — in that she was not disturbed by the false plausibility of my interpretation and so quickly saw what was to be seen (which I certainly had not seen until she said it) — than by the dream itself: by which the joy that was to come to that holy woman so long after was foretold so long before for the relief of her present anguish" (*Confessions*, Book Three, XI, p. 56).

Though deeply moved by Monica's interpretation of her dream, Augustine was not yet ready to surrender. He was then at the height of his proselyting efforts as a Manichaean. He was not satisfied merely to adhere to the sect; he also wanted to spread its teachings. In another book he relates that he had even led his protector Romanianus into error. In his *Confessions*, he concludes the passage with the following lines:

"Nine years were to follow in which I lay tossing in the mud of that deep pit and the darkness of its falsity, though I often tried to rise and only fell the more heavily. All this time this chaste, God-fearing and sober widow — for such You love — was all the more cheered up with hope. Yet she did not relax her weeping and mourning. She did not cease to pray at every hour and bewail me to You, and her prayers found entry into Your sight. But for all that, You allowed me still to toss helplessly in that darkness" (*Confessions*, Book Three, XI, p. 56).

If there is any conclusion that we can draw from the above example, it is that we must not expect a single prayer uttered distractedly and on the run, so to speak, to be infallibly answered. True, the Gospel clearly says: "Ask, and you will receive…. Knock, and it will be opened to you" (Matthew 7:7). And yet the emphasis of Jesus Christ's words suggests how insistent we must be in our prayers.

The triumph of faith consists in persevering in our petitions. Above all else, Monica persevered in fervent prayer. And that is why her prayer was finally answered far beyond her wildest expectations.

Monica consults a bishop

There was great merit in Monica's perseverance.

We might say it was her faith's response to a secret grace from God. For, as we have already pointed out, while God made her wait until the moment He had decreed to answer her prayers, He also granted her encouragements and maternal intuitions that helped buoy her hopes.

The dream of the wooden rule had been one of these secret encouragements. She also received another, which Augustine recounts in his *Confessions*. He tells us that in her distress she consulted the best educated clergymen she knew. She even approached a bishop who had a profound knowledge of the Scriptures, for it was on Scripture that the Manichaeans based their principal objections to the Catholic faith. She told the bishop about her son's spiritual and theological problems, and begged him to speak to him and refute the errors into which he had fallen. She explained that she hoped in this way to bring him back to the true faith.

After the bishop had thought the matter over he decided he could not intervene, and yet he did

not want to add to this mother's affliction. According
to Augustine's account:

"He told her that I was not yet ripe for teaching
because I was all puffed up with the newness of my
heresy and had already upset a number of insuf-
ficiently skilled people with certain questions — as
she had, in fact, told him. 'But,' said he, 'let him
alone. Only pray to the Lord for him: he will himself
discover by reading what his error is and how great
his impiety....' When he had told her this, my mother
would not be satisfied but urged him with repeated
entreaties and floods of tears to see me and discuss
with me. He, losing patience, said: '*Go your way;
as sure as you live, it is impossible that the son of
these tears should perish.*' In the conversations we
had afterwards, she often said she had accepted this
answer as if it were from heaven" (*Confessions*,
Book Three, XII, pp. 56-57).

The bishop was right. Faith could only penetrate
a soul well prepared to receive it, a soul made trac-
table by humility.

Augustine was still far from possessing such
humility. His mother sadly watched him harden his
heart as he yielded to his passions and his worldly
ambitions. To his mind, Manichaeism had the advantage of promising salvation to its followers in good
standing. To those who thirsted for purity, Manichaeism declared its elect lived in perfect chastity
and perpetual abstinence. On the other hand, if
one wanted to continue a life of vice, it affirmed that
while auditors were not obliged to practice the pen-
ance demanded of the elect, they would be saved
along with them. So Augustine remained an auditor
in the sect. In order to exonerate himself and to wash
away his personal sins, he had only to offer food to
the elect. Their sound digestion would liberate him
from the purifying angels.

This is how he described his life during that
period:

"Throughout that nine-year period, from my nineteenth year to my twenty-eighth, I was astray myself and led others astray, was deceived and deceived others in various forms of self-assertion, publicly by the teaching of what are called the liberal arts, privately under the false name of religion; in the one proud, in the other superstitious, in both vain. On the one side of my life I pursued the emptiness of popular glory and the applause of spectators, with competition for prize poems and strife for garlands of straw and the vanity of stage shows and untempered lusts; on the other side I was striving to be made clean of all this same filth, by bearing food to those who were called elect and holy, that in the factory of their own stomachs they should turn it into angels and deities by whom I was to be set free" *(Confessions,* Book Four, I, p. 61).

Augustine's attitude bore no resemblance to the holy virtue of humility. As far as he was concerned, only one thing mattered: Fame! He would later see it as vanity of vanities.

Sometime around the year 380, Augustine dedicated two philosophical treatises to an orator named Hiereus, then famous in Rome but now completely forgotten. He did it not out of friendship or in gratitude for a service rendered, for he did not even know the man. What he hoped was that Hiereus would compliment him on his writings and thus enhance his reputation.

In another work entitled *On the Usefulness of Faith,* Augustine described his state of mind at that time:

"I thought only about the beauty of a wife, about the pageantry of riches, the vanity of honors and all the other deadly and pernicious lusts. I did not for a moment stop desiring and hoping for all these things at the time I was listening with great attention to the Manichaeans."

And yet, referring to the distinction between the elect who claimed to be so ascetic and mortified and the auditors to whom everything was permitted, he added:

"However I do not blame all my weaknesses on their teachings, for I admit that they, too, carefully warn their followers to avoid them."

The Manichaeans deceived many by the apparent virtue of their elect.

Let us cite an example that will show us one of the reasons for their success and introduce a personage who was to play a very important part in Augustine's life. Obviously, this person was also well known to Monica. We are referring to Augustine's intimate friend Alypius, born in Tagaste and one of his disciples. Monica must have held him in high regard because of his friendship with her son and his unfeigned admiration for him. In fact, she may well have looked upon him as another son. Now Alypius had been deceived by the outward austerity of the Manichaean elect. To quote Augustine:

"Alypius had been lured into this superstition just as I had. He liked their display of a continence that he imagined genuine and authentic, whereas it was false and deceptive. They looked about for well-born persons to lead them to perdition, for such had not yet learned how to penetrate the depths of virtue and were easily dazzled by false appearances."

First glimmers of light

The reason we are describing Augustine's spiritual evolution in such detail is that his life paralleled his mother's, and was in a sense her life's work. For her prayers secretly guided the course of her son's rise to greatness.

Monica had been told that if her son Augustine read the books of the Manichaeans, he would finally come to see their errors. And this is precisely what happened. Alypius, as we have said, was attracted to Manichaeism by the outward appearances of feigned virtue. Augustine, for his part, was fascinated by the false brilliance of their knowledge displayed in the works of Manes, for instance. But when he compared Manes with the philosophers whom he also read with careful attention, he seemed to discover omissions and doubtful affirmations that bred mistrust.

Manes, being a good Babylonian, had spoken much of the stars. In Augustine's day the knowledge of astronomy was advancing. When he compared Manes' theories with those of the Greek "philosophers" who were also concerned with astronomy, he realized that Manes had made enormous errors in calculation regarding the equinoxes, solstices, eclipses, and other phenomena of like nature. He therefore quickly turned to his Manichaean teachers in Carthage asking for explanations. None of them could offer a satisfactory answer. They were totally unaware of the difficulties he set before them. With unruffled assurance they answered him that their bishop, Faustus by name, had a thorough grasp of all wisdom. Indeed, when the bishop came to Carthage, they said, he could easily set Augustine's mind at rest about all the matters that were troubling him. So Augustine was simply asked to await his coming patiently. In fact, they spoke so highly of Faustus that it was hard not to accept the infallibility of this great Manichaean dignitary.

It was to be many years before Augustine had a chance to personally confront the Manichaean bishop. Meanwhile, he continued to read and study. Despite the turmoil of his passions, his meditations at this period of his life were already on a lofty plane. He was deeply interested in understanding the meaning of *divine substance!* Is this not the most noble subject about which any man can reflect?

Monica had spoken to her son about God from his earliest childhood, as the *All-powerful and Invisible Being* who made all things and whom all must worship and love. But now Augustine wanted to know more about this Being. He could not shake off the obsession that the only real things are those we touch, see, hear, and contact through our bodily senses. Outside of these material realities, Augustine mistakenly believed, there were only imaginings and nothingness. The Manichaeans had fallen into the same error, which is none other than the most vulgar and childish materialism.

"Tossing about feverishly in my deprivation of truth, I sought You, O my God, not by the light of the intellect that makes me superior to the animals, but through my bodily senses.... I did not know that God is a pure spirit, who has neither limbs nor parts, neither length, nor breadth, nor extension."

That is also a definition of our intellect. It has neither spatial dimensions, nor bodily articulations. For the Manichaeans, the solution was very simple. The divine substance was quite literally the sun. Hence, it was a bodily substance.

That is why Augustine took so many years to extricate himself from Manichaean materialism. As he saw it at that time, God could only be—as he himself expressed it—"a luminous and immense body, of which he, Augustine, was only a fragment."

So Augustine professed a kind of materialistic pantheism. When he thought about it in later years, he commented: *"O excesses of perversity!"* Rather, it was an excess of metaphysical ignorance and error. He was to be delivered from this primitive thinking only by the Platonic philosophers whom he discovered in Milan after leaving Carthage. The details of this period of Augustine's life will be told in the next chapter.

6

Monica Returns to Tagaste

The return to Tagaste

*T*his portion of St. Augustine's life could be called his "Carthage period." It lasted about twelve years, from 371 to 383. But his life in Carthage was interrupted by a year's stay in Tagaste, from 374 to 375. Monica understandably returned with her son to his native city, and remained there until she finally went to join him in Milan during the decisive years of his conversion.

Augustine had completed his studies at Carthage in 374, when he was twenty years old. It has sometimes been thought that he had first intended to practice law. This does not seem likely. Nowhere does he speak of engaging in legal studies. He devoted himself first to literature, and then to philosophy. Later, under the influence of Manichaeism, he studied astronomy, which soon degenerated—as was often the case in those days—into astrology, i.e., an effort to predict the future by means of a study of the conjunctions of the stars and planets.

When his studies were completed, he returned to Tagaste where he opened a school of literature. He became a teacher of grammar and rhetoric. Among his students were his friend Alypius, Licentius, the son of his protector Romanianus, as well as other young men. It is interesting to note that even at that early stage of his life he developed great and lasting friendships. He hungered for friends, and the group that now formed around him in Tagaste was closely bound by ties of friendship. Alypius would never leave him. Augustine must have had such a magnetic, outgoing, and loving personality that it was impossible not to be drawn to him. These facts had their effect on Monica, too. She came to share her son's friendships and to look on his friends as her own sons.

Let us consider the powerful hold friendship had on Augustine.

Death of a friend

Among the friends who had returned from Carthage with Augustine, there was one whose name we do not know, about whom Augustine wrote in stirring language in his *Confessions*. Let us read Augustine's own account:

"During the period in which I first began to teach in the town of my birth, I had found a very dear friend, who was pursuing similar studies. He was about my own age, and was now coming, as I was, to the very flowering-time of young manhood. He had indeed grown up with me as a child and we had gone to school together and played together. Neither in those earlier days nor indeed in the later time of which I now speak was he a friend in the truest meaning of friendship: for there is no true friendship unless You weld it between souls that cleave together through the charity which is shed in our hearts by the Holy Ghost who is given to us. Yet it had become a friendship very dear to us, made the warmer by the ardor of studies pursued together. I had turned him from the true faith — in which being little more than a boy he was not deeply grounded — towards those superstitious and soul-destroying errors that my mother bewailed in me. With me he went astray in error, and my soul could not be without him" (Book Four, IV, pp. 64-65).

Here we discover one of the bonds that chained him to Manichaeism. In his neophyte's enthusiasm, he had propagated heresy around him. His very conquests were an incentive to hold fast to the false sect. The reflection of his convictions which he saw in his friends strengthened their hold upon his own mind.

Now, an unexpected event took place that threw Augustine into an ocean of salutary reflection. His friend became ill. Soon a fever, of which we know neither the name nor the nature, brought him to death's door. Augustine remained by his friend's side constantly, watching him toss on his bed of pain, bathed in a mortal sweat. All hope was given up for his recovery.

Now, like Augustine, this young man had been inscribed in the register of catechumens, probably since infancy. It was the custom to baptize catechumens in danger of death, to prepare them to appear before their Judge. The dying youth had lost consciousness. Augustine was present at his baptism. But deep within himself, he felt only scorn for these few drops of water poured out on a man deprived of all sensation. He was confident that if his friend did get well, everyone would see the baptismal ritual had made no difference whatever in his ideas. But Augustine was forced to admit:

"It turned out very differently. The fever left him and he recovered. As soon as I could speak to him — which was as soon as he could speak to me, for I had not left him and indeed we depended too much upon each other — I began to mock, assuming that he would join me in mocking, the baptism which he had received when he had neither sense nor feeling. For by now he had been told of it. But he looked at me as if I had been his deadly enemy, and, in a burst of independence that startled me, warned me that if I wished to continue his friend I must cease that kind of talk. I was stupefied and deeply perturbed" (*Confessions*, Book Four, IV, pp. 65-66).

In his amazement, Augustine was silent. He assumed that his friend was still suffering from the effects of his illness. He decided to wait until he had begun to convalesce before reasoning with him so as to draw him back into his Manichaean errors. However, things turned out differently. The sick youth did not recover. Within a very few days the fever rekindled, and he died.

Now Augustine was crushed with sorrow:

"My heart was black with grief. Whatever I looked upon had the air of death. My native place was a prison-house and my home a strange unhappiness. The things we had done together became sheer torment without him. My eyes were restless looking for him, but he was not there. I hated all places because he was not in them. They could not say, 'He will come soon,' as they would in his life when he was absent. I became a great enigma to myself and I was forever asking my soul why it was sad and why it disquieted me so sorely. And my soul knew not what to answer me.... I had no delight but in tears, for tears had taken the place my friend had held in the love of my heart" (Book Four, IV, p. 66).

In vain did Monica try to console her son. In vain did his other friends do everything in their power to support and distract him. His sorrow, un-relieved by any religious hope, was beyond remedy:

"I raged and sighed and wept and was in tor-ment, unable to rest, unable to think. I bore my soul all broken and bleeding and loathing to be borne by me; and I could find nowhere to set it down to rest. Not in shady groves, nor in mirth and music, nor in perfumed gardens, nor in formal banquets, nor in the delights of bedroom and bed, nor in books, nor in poetry could it find peace. I hated all things, hated the very light itself; and all that was not he was painful and wearisome, save only my tears: for in them alone did I find a little peace" (*Confessions*, Book Four, VII, p. 68).

Augustine's emotional turmoil was so intense that Tagaste became unbearable to him. He came to hate the streets where he had strolled with his lost friend. Everything around him aroused revulsion and despair. He could not stop mulling over the death of his friend.

"I wondered that other mortals should live when he was dead whom I had loved as if he would never die; and I marvelled still more that he should be dead and I, his other self, living still. Rightly has a friend been called 'the half of my soul.' For I thought of my soul and his soul as one soul in two bodies; and my life was a horror to me because I would not live halved. And it may be that I feared to die lest thereby he should die wholly whom I had loved so deeply" (Book Four, VI, p. 68).

Augustine's grief was consuming him, and Moni-ca sadly watched her son languish. She feared for his health, which had never been robust. It soon be-came evident that Augustine could not remain in Tagaste. But where would he go? There was still only Carthage, which, for Monica, was the city of perdition. But he must leave his native town without delay. Perhaps his professional activities would save him from the brink of despair. Monica therefore consented to his departure.

Augustine began to plan to open a school of rhetoric in Carthage. The very thought of it revived his ambitions and his ingrained thirst for renown.

When Augustine left Tagaste Monica did not follow him. She remained behind, devoting herself more than ever to prayer and weeping. No doubt, mother and son exchanged letters frequently. They probably also took advantage of every opportunity to be together, especially during vacation periods.

We shall soon come back to Augustine and his new life. But let us now turn to Monica, and reflect on her virtues. Eight years were to elapse from the time of Augustine's return to Carthage in 375, until his departure for Rome in 383. For Augustine these would be years of hard work and growing disenchantment. For Monica, they were years of ever more intense prayer.

A stirring portrait

Monica's life during this period has been eloquently depicted for us by her son in his *Confessions:*

"But would You, O God of mercy, despise the contrite and humble heart of that chaste and pious widow, so generous in almsgiving, so ready in the service of Your saints, who let no day pass without attending the sacrifice at Your altar, and came twice a day with never an exception, morning and evening, to Your church, not to listen to idle tales and the gossip of the women but that she might hear You in Your discourses, and You her in her prayers?" (Book Five, IX, p. 95)

This certainly gives us a picture of Monica's life. Her prolonged, silent meditation is what we have come to call "mental prayer." In short, Monica lived in intimate contact with her God, in a rapture of love, filled with heavenly lights and high aspirations, a life of faith and trust.

Yes, Monica was eminently a woman of prayer, a woman who lived a very lofty interior life. Nowadays, we would say she was a mystic.

Various texts collected by the Bollandists[1] for use in the Augustinian breviaries describe Monica's holiness in greater detail, but along the same lines as the brief summary given above by Augustine. Let us reread some of these texts.

First, there is reference to Monica's love for fasting.

"So great was the grace by which this servant of Christ surpassed all others in fasting, that when she sat down to eat, she did so only as though to take a bitter medicine!"

Her words were always restrained, modest, and wise:

"Never a profane word...but in all her conversations, she called Christ to mind!"

Above all, Monica practiced charity toward the unfortunate and the poor. She had always been charitable. During her husband's lifetime and as long as her son Augustine had required extensive financial help, she had been obliged to restrain her generous impulses. But Augustine was now earning his own way. Monica even reduced her own style of living with her two remaining children, so that she could give more to the less fortunate. Better still, she gave of herself. She knew that a kind act, a delicate attention, intelligent and devoted care do much more good to others than money. She made up her mind to be the servant of the poor. One of the breviary texts even says: "She was called the mother of the poor rather than the servant of the poor."

An ancient hymn attributed to Adam of Saint-Victor in the twelfth century says of her:

She served the needy,
And fed them in Christ;

1. See footnote 2, p. 25.

Known as the mother of the poor,
Taking care of the infirm,
She washed and bound their wounds,
And cleansed them of filth!

There was not a work of charity to which she did not devote herself. For her, these were works of piety. Another text says she had a special gift for consoling widows as well as persons who were unhappy in their marriages.

But Monica's good works and contemplation were rooted in the Holy Sacrifice of the Mass, or as we say today, the Eucharistic celebration. As Augustine has mentioned, she "let no day pass without attending the sacrifice at Your altar." Indeed, she did more than merely "attend" Mass. She participated in it and united herself to Christ in Communion. At Mass she made sincere efforts to increase the love that already filled her heart and poured out incessant prayers for the endangered soul of her beloved son.

It was during such privileged moments that Augustine's words about her were fulfilled: "I have no words to express the love she had for me, and with how much more anguish she was now in spiritual travail of me than when she had borne me in the flesh!" (*Confessions*, Book Five, IX, p. 95)

And how could her prayers fail to be answered since she asked for her son neither earthly successes, gold, silver, nor honors, but solely the salvation of his soul?

The ancient ascetic authors often referred with admiration to what was known as "the gift of tears," much less common today. It would seem that Monica was granted this rare gift in an eminent degree.

But can we discern in Augustine's life some indication that God was answering Monica's insistent prayers?

Augustine is the first to tell us that his mother's prayers saved him. But he indicates that it happened by "wonderful and hidden ways." Elsewhere he cries out: "For Your hand, O my God, in the secret of Your Providence did not desert my soul...and You did act with me in marvelous ways" *(Confessions,* Book Five, VII, pp. 91-92).

We shall now try to describe Augustine's spiritual evolution in the light of God's response to Monica's prayers and tears.

Augustine's experiences

One fact emerges very clearly from the *Confessions:* Augustine thirsted for the truth. Although he didn't realize it at the time, this was a very great grace. He was not satisfied with what he knew, with what the Manichaeans had taught him. He searched, he yearned to know, his spirit was restlessly questing.

Without these vast aspirations, without his hunger for the whole truth, he would have remained engulfed in his early errors. God had endowed him with an open, receptive mind. This favor from heaven is perhaps the most divine of dispositions. Even for those who are sure they possess the truth, this thirst for a deeper understanding and a more perfect grasp of the truth is an indispensable attitude. Woe to those who are too easily satisfied! There is always more to learn, to meditate upon, to yearn for, and to beseech.

Augustine was searching. We can agree with him that his mother's prayers had earned this favor for him.

In the second place, he continued to make rapid progress in discovering the truth for which he was searching. For he had come to understand that it wasn't the beautiful words in which thoughts were couched that mattered, but the meaning of the thoughts themselves. This may seem elementary to us. But for Augustine, it was a high hurdle. He delighted in beautiful language. He was enthralled by eloquence. He was constantly studying the principles of rhetoric so as to teach them to others.

It was about this time, in the year 380, that he wrote his first treatise, which he sent to Hiereus in Rome. Actually, this writing was lost, and even Augustine had no copy of it at the time he wrote his *Confessions*, in or about 400 A.D.

But above and beyond the beauty of the words themselves, Augustine was beginning to understand that he must admire the beauty of the ideas that words expressed, and this beauty was to be identified with truth itself. This second grace complemented the first. He had a love of truth, but now he was searching for it above and beyond the beauty of words.

A third advantage was that Augustine was being taught sound lessons of Catholic doctrine. This came about especially through a man named Helpidius who happened to be in Carthage when Augustine was there. Helpidius had been giving public lectures in the city, and Augustine, always keenly interested in lectures of this sort, had been present. Helpidius had shown that Manichaeism was full of contradictions, and also explicitly contrary to very firmly-established texts of both the Old and the New Testaments.

Augustine knew very little of the Scriptures at that time, and was very much impressed by Helpidius' arguments. He remembered that the Bible's simple language had turned him away from it. Now he knew he must beware of beautiful language when it is empty of meaning. And he began to wonder whether the Scriptures he had scoffed at might not indeed contain the truth for which he thirsted.

So Helpidius' lectures made a profound impression on Augustine and caused him salutary concern. He had not been completely shaken, but he was certainly much less sure of himself. He was beginning to formulate doubts as to the truth of Manichaeism, but bolstered his morale with the thought that Faustus, the bishop of the Manichaeans, was soon expected in Carthage. This man, he had been assured, had an answer to every question because he knew everything. So Augustine decided to wait until he was finally sure before making any public statement. This attitude of patient expectation was a far cry from his intemperate proselyting of earlier years.

Little by little the road was opening up before him, and the way made smooth. Such is often God's way. We shall soon inquire why God's providence made Augustine travel such a tortuous path, in spite of his mother's holy impatience. The best answer is that the whole future career of Augustine the great Doctor of the universal Church was being prepared, without the slightest realization on his part, through the experiences of this troubled period.

Faustus the Manichaean

The day finally came when the Manichaeans announced to Augustine and to all their followers that Faustus, their much-vaunted bishop, was coming. A veritable legend had grown up around him. It was said he had sacrificed everything to his love of truth. He had left his father and mother, his wife and children, and even his native land, to devote himself to his apostolate. He scorned gold and silver, living in poverty. He was gentle and peace-loving toward everyone. In a word, he was a saint in the fullest sense of the word. At least that is what his dazzled disciples kept telling everybody. Augustine was perhaps more eager than anyone to see him, meet him, and hear him speak.

Monica, on the other hand, wondered fearfully whether this man whom the Catholics called "the devil's trap" might not drag her son to the depths of hell. It is not unlikely that when she learned about

Faustus' impending arrival, she went to Carthage, where she probably visited her son as often as possible.

What was going to happen? This was to be another decisive moment in Augustine's life.

At first, Augustine was enchanted. Faustus was really a fine man. He was modest and dignified in mien. Above all, he expressed himself in perfect language. In later years Augustine was to say that when he compared Faustus to another great orator, St. Ambrose, he had to admit Faustus was a more elegant, mellow, and compelling speaker. Obviously, from the point of view of subject matter, the two men were worlds apart.

To quote Augustine: "I was delighted with the sweetness of Ambrose's discourses. But even though they were sounder and more learned, they did not have the charm or power of those given by Faustus."

But after the first flush of enthusiasm, Augustine, as was now his custom, began to reflect. Faustus spoke well, but was he saying anything new? Nothing, absolutely nothing. "I found him a pleasant man of pleasant speech, who rolled off the same sort of things the others had said but with far greater charm" (Confessions, Book Five, VI). Faustus' discourses were beautiful vases, but they were empty!

When Augustine listened to Faustus during his public lectures, he quivered with impatience. He wanted to interrupt him, ask him questions, demand more complete explanations. But that was not the usual practice. Augustine therefore asked his friends to obtain a private audience for him with the master.

The request was granted. If, as is probable, Monica was then in Carthage, she must have redoubled her prayers for her son on the eve of his meeting with Faustus.

Augustine came to the audience surrounded by his closest friends, as eager as he to know what Faustus could teach them. Augustine has given us an exact

account of this memorable encounter in his *Confessions*, as well as in a special treatise entitled *Contra Faustum* ("Reply to Faustus"). With his very
first questions, Augustine became aware that Faustus was not a philosopher. In fact, even his training
in literature was quite limited.

Faustus had probably read a few of Cicero's
treatises or discourses, a few passages from Seneca,
some Latin poems, and above all the principal books
of the Manichaean sect. As he was constantly prac-
ticing the art of rhetoric for which he had natural
aptitudes, he expressed himself with genuine charm.
However, his words did not express deeply-held
convictions. It was all on the surface.

Augustine came away from this first meeting not
a little disconcerted. It was hard for a mind like his
to have waited so long, hoped for so much, and then
encounter complete emptiness. But he did not give
up. He consulted Faustus on questions that the local
Manichaeans had left unanswered. As we have already mentioned, these were problems relating to
astronomy and astrology. Manes had spoken of these
matters like a man who was totally ignorant of their
meaning.

What would Faustus say? For Augustine, this
was the decisive test. From the start, Faustus declared frankly and with perfect equanimity that he
was incompetent to answer. This was a point in his
favor, to Augustine's mind. He wrote:

"He knew that he did not know these things,
and he was not ashamed to admit it; he was not one
of those talkative people — of whom I had suffered
many — who would undertake to teach me, and say
nothing. For he had a heart, which though it was
not right towards God, was reasonably cautious in
the matter of himself. He was not entirely ignorant
of his own ignorance.... Even for this I liked him
better" (*Confessions*, Book Five, VII, p. 91).

All things considered, it was a hard blow. Augustine was obliged to draw the logical conclusions. He was completely disillusioned. If this man so highly vaunted by his followers could not tell him anything, no one else could.

Augustine did not pursue his thinking to the point of agreeing that the Catholic Church was right. That road was still closed to him. He had told himself once and for all, he thought, that while the teachings of the Church might be good for a fine woman like Monica, they were not acceptable to a disciplined and inquiring mind such as his. Or so he thought. Soon afterward, Augustine fell into the skepticism of the "Academics," as they were then called. For the time being, his decision was as follows:

"All my effort and determination to make progress in the sect simply fell away through my coming to know this man [Faustus]. Not that I separated myself from them entirely; but simply, not finding anything better than the course upon which I had somehow or other stumbled, I decided to look no further for the time unless something more desirable should chance to appear" (Book Five, VII, p. 91).

Later on Augustine would finally realize this salutary disappointment was another of God's graces to him, won by his mother's tireless supplications.

"Thus Faustus, who had been a snare that brought death to many, did without his knowledge or will begin to unbind the snare that held me" (Book Five, VII, p. 91).

Then, turning to God, as he does throughout his *Confessions*, he wrote these stirring words:

"For Your hand, O my God, in the secret of Your providence did not desert my soul; from the blood of my mother's heart, sacrifice for me was offered You day and night by her tears, and You did act with me in marvelous ways. For it was You, my God, who did do it" (Book Five, VII, pp. 91-92).

We shall look further into these "marvelous ways" in the even more astonishing developments in our saints' lives which we are about to relate.

7

Monica's Great Desolation

Augustine's departure

Monica had reason to rejoice over the negative outcome of Augustine's encounter with Faustus. However, she was painfully surprised to learn of her son's decision to leave Carthage and go to Rome.

Augustine claimed he had very serious reasons for going to Rome. He did not hesitate to let his mother know what they were, not realizing she would want to follow him to Italy. And this was something he wanted to avoid at all costs.

His reasons for leaving Carthage were these: The students of Carthage had always been fractious and noisy. As one of them, Augustine had never taken part in their vulgar and rather barbaric practices. It was common knowledge that bands of students forced their way into courses for which they had not been enrolled, just to cause a disturbance. They would burst into a class and harass the serious students or even the professor with all sorts of pranks. And if they were reprimanded, even if the police were called, they insisted they were just following the customs of their country.

It had taken Augustine a long time to notice all this. He may finally have been the victim of some extraordinary insolence that he has never described in detail. Perhaps, too, after waiting so long for Faustus and then being disappointed in him, he may have thought it best to seek a new theater of activity.

What more beautiful theater than Rome? Rome was the capital of the Empire in the West. It had retained intact the prestige of past greatness. As we have mentioned, Augustine had already dedicated several treatises to a famous Roman orator, including one entitled *De Pulchro et Apto* (On the Good and Fitting). He supposed his writings had made some impression on the Romans. Besides, his friends in Carthage told him he would have a better chance of success in Rome than in his native Africa. In any event, he looked forward to having more disciplined and industrious students than those of Carthage.

What was his surprise when he told his plans to his mother! She insisted she would either do everything in her power to prevent his departure, or else follow him wherever he went. Touched as he was by his mother's devotion, he could not help finding it tyrannical, and to say the least, cumbersome. He made up his mind to leave without her.

But for all his efforts to keep his preparations for the journey secret, he could not hide them from his mother. Monica never left him for a moment. When he went down to the port in the company of a friend to board a ship sailing for Rome, Monica followed him, clinging to his arm as though she wanted to keep him with her always. What could he do? He decided to deceive his mother:

"I lied to my mother, and such a mother, and so got away from her. But this also You have mercifully forgiven me, O God!" (*Confessions*, Book Five, VIII, p. 93)

Augustine's lie consisted in telling his mother that the ship could not sail until the next day because of unfavorable winds. Monica refused to leave the port, but went to a nearby chapel dedicated to St. Cyprian. Instead of sleeping, this holy mother prayed as was her custom. Augustine asks:

"And what was she praying for, O my God, with all those tears but that You should not allow me to sail! But You saw deeper and granted the essential of her prayer: You did not do what she was at that moment asking, that You might do the thing she was always asking. The wind blew and filled our sails and the shore dropped from our sight" (*Confessions*, Book Five, VIII, pp. 93-94).

It was in Italy that Augustine would be converted and his mother's prayers finally answered. But for the moment Monica was distraught over her son's deception.

Desolation

Frantic with grief, Monica wandered along the shore, complaining that God had not heard her prayers. She would have taken any ship sailing for Rome to catch up with her fugitive son. She had wanted to share the dangers of the sea with him, and the even greater dangers that might well be in store for him in the capital of the Empire. To quote the *Confessions:*

"You seemed to treat her tears so lightly, when in fact You were using my own desires to snatch me away for the healing of those desires, and were justly punishing her own too earthly affection for me with the scourge of grief. For she loved to have me with her, as is the way of mothers but far more than most mothers; and she did not realize what joys You would bring her from my going away" (Book Five, VIII, p. 94).

But what would she do now? Since she could not follow her son, she had to return to Tagaste. But here her virtue shown forth. Just as she did not stop loving this son whom she had every reason to condemn, so she did not stop praying though it seemed God paid little attention to her prayers.

Monica's mother love on the one hand and her faith in her God on the other were two unshakable pillars of strength. And so, as Augustine puts it, she continued to pray and to "shed those rivers of tears that covered the place where she prayed each day."

Monica waited patiently for news from her son. We have no record of any letters he may have written her. We do know, however, that she did join him as soon as it became possible. This means he must have let her know he had arrived safely in Rome and where she could reach him. He may even have apologized to her for his sudden departure by inventing some unlikely reason for it.

Let us now follow Augustine to Rome. Thanks to his mother's prayers he was to have experiences there that would prove very precious to him in his future ministry. This might be an opportune place to make a few comments of our own.

Preparation

Augustine said that God saw things "from a higher vantage point" than he. It is very evident to us now, but it may have been hard to understand at the time. What he meant was that our prayers are not always answered immediately and literally, but are sometimes answered later in a higher way. We find this doctrine implied throughout the *Confessions*.

We know now that Augustine was predestined to become the "Doctor of the West." So it is easy for us to see the reason for the "preparation" God demanded of him, which was to answer Monica's prayers and tears *in a higher way*.

In looking over the list of Augustine's writings, we find those he directed first of all against the Manichaeans, and Faustus in particular, then against the "Academics," that is, the Agnostics or Sceptics, whose ranks he was to join before being converted to the true faith.

Speaking from his own personal experience, he could be much more eloquent, and surer in his arguments against error and heresy, thus preserving his own and future generations from their evils. As we see it, that is the reason for Augustine's countless detours in his journey to God. It was a painful novitiate, we might say, a novitiate decreed by Providence and whose lessons would remain in his blood until he died.

How can we explain the fact that Augustine's life finally bore such abundant fruit as to enrich all succeeding generations? The answer is to be found in his long and arduous preparation during which he searched for the truth. Even more important, his mother prayed so hard when he did not pray, shed so many tears when he was straying far from the path of truth and goodness, that in the end all these factors combined, under God's ever-merciful gaze, to produce the great saint we now honor as St. Augustine, Bishop and Doctor.

Augustine often repeated that his mother had borne him twice: first in the flesh, and afterwards in the spirit. He did not hesitate to say that the second childbirth was perhaps far more painful than the first.

We know that Augustine became the "Doctor of grace." Now, grace is one of the most mysterious areas of Christian theology. Paul had been the doctor of grace among the apostles. He, too, had had an impassioned and unsettled youth, and been prepared by his experiences to follow the secret but powerful inspirations of grace. Is this not the explanation of Augustine's life and of his mother's trials? Nothing happens unless God wills or permits it. But in a peerless destiny such as Augustine's, extraordinary events are to be expected. In fact, it would be surprising were it otherwise.

We now follow Augustine to Rome, where he was to remain only a year.

Rome in 383

Strangely enough, when Augustine came to Rome in the year 383, probably after the vacation period or at the start of the scholastic year, he saw absolutely nothing of the Catholic Rome of that day. In his *Confessions* he makes no mention of the reigning Pope who was St. Damasus (366-384), or of the catacombs where so many martyrs were now being honored. Neither did he refer to a certain lecturer named Jerome who was enjoying great success in the Catholic circles of the capital, with the Pope's approbation. Jerome was already the spiritual director of the most eminent Christian ladies of Rome, those who belonged to the oldest families of the Roman patrician class. Among them were Paula, Fabiola, Eustochium, Marcella, and so many others.

Augustine obviously knew nothing of the Catholic life of Rome. He associated only with the Manichaeans. The members of the sect in Carthage had sent him an introduction to one of their number in Rome, who invited him to stay at his home. And yet he does admit that he did think of consulting a Catholic scholar about Scriptural questions he had discussed with the Manichaeans and on which he had found them wanting more than once. Why didn't he follow through in his quest for information? Indeed, Jerome was the most highly qualified man of his time to answer his questions and dispel all his doubts. For whatever reason, Augustine never approached him. Perhaps his prejudices against the Catholic Church were still too deep-seated. Perhaps, too, he encountered too much prejudice on the part of the Manichaeans with whom he consorted.

At any rate, Augustine has told us that in his perplexity, he began to doubt everything. For now he could see at close range how the followers of Manes lived, and realized that the virtue of their *Elect* was greatly overrated. In fact, their mores were as shameful and corrupt as they claimed they were pure and above reproach. Deep in his mind, he began to think that the Academics or Agnostics were probably right after all!

Augustine among the Academics

The Academics were the distant but decadent disciples of the Academy, the school founded seven hundred years earlier by the great Plato. The Academics maintained that the truth is beyond the reach of the human intellect, that nothing can be known with absolute certainty, and hence the best attitude is one of permanent doubt.

But that is more easily said than done. Man has an ingrained need for the truth. If he cannot attain the truth, a chasm of emptiness opens up within him that can cause him acute, indeed, unbearable suffering. Augustine was a man who could never be satisfied to remain in a state of insoluble doubt. Although he probably threw himself into his teaching to try to forget, an ever-growing sadness took hold of him.

This depression seems to have been the cause of a sickness that soon brought him to death's door. Here are his own words:

"Rome welcomed me with the scourge of bodily illness, and I very nearly went to hell bearing all the weight of deadly sins which I had committed against You and myself and other men, over and above the bond of original sin whereby we all die in Adam. For You had not yet forgiven any of my sins in Christ" (*Confessions*, Book Five, IX, p. 94).

Even in this extremity Augustine had no thought of receiving baptism. He has declared that he had degenerated so far from the faith of his childhood that he did not even think of repeating what he had done when he was a child. For then, when seriously ill, he had begged to be baptized. Now he was in Rome, far from his mother's vigilant gaze, about to die without a priest, without Christ, without God.

"For where should I have gone if I had departed then save to fire and torments such as my deeds deserved in the justice of Your ordinance?... For great as that peril had been I did not ask for Your baptism" (*Confessions*, Book Five, IX, p. 95).

Later on, he would realize he had been preserved without knowing it. Preserved how and by whom? Yes, we already know. By his mother. There are few such clear examples in the history of the Church.

"My mother was far away and knew nothing of my illness, but she prayed on for me. You who are present everywhere heard her where she was and had compassion on me where I was, so that I recovered the health of my body.... I have no words to express the love she had for me" (Book Five, IX, p. 94).

And he concludes, addressing himself to God:

"I had grown rooted into my shame; and new in folly scorned Your healing precepts, who had saved me from double death in my sins. Had my mother's heart been pierced by *that* wound, it would never have been made whole" (Book Five, IX, p. 95).

At the very moment Monica's prayers seemed fruitless, at least as far as the precise answer she was expecting, they were mightily influencing the course of Augustine's life, directing it toward God.

We can be assured that this is always so. Our entreaties are heard, for God is always open to our requests even though His response may not seem to agree with our desires. In His plans, days and months that seem so long to us are really only a very short interval of time because He is eternal.

Augustine's disgust with Rome

Augustine remained in Rome only for one scholastic year, probably from the fall of 383 to the fall of 384.

He soon became disgusted with Rome for several reasons. It had not offered him the success he had so confidently expected there. As a young rhetorician fresh from Africa, he had not found acceptance in the great imperial city. He was completely ignored. He had opened a school, but it apparently attracted few students, and these were of a very different caliber from what he had hoped.

Augustine's Roman students were much less boisterous and undisciplined than those of Carthage. They did not burst into classrooms and topple the furniture over, but they showed little courtesy and less appreciation for the trouble their teachers took to instruct them. Quite a few of them dropped the course when it was time to pay the professor's fee. They were penny-pinching and frivolous. Augustine had been warned that "at a given moment a number of students plan together to cheat their master of his fees, and go off to some other master. They are utterly faithless and hold justice cheap, compared with love of money" (*Confessions*, Book Five, XII, p. 99). To Augustine's mind, such behavior was even more shocking than the more blatant ways of the African students. It was a form of swindling, a denial of justice, a lack of honor.

In addition to these troubles, Augustine was greatly disappointed in the Manichaeans. He lodged with one of them, and had been recommended to the Manichaeans of Rome by their co-members in Carthage. As a result, he was accepted not only by the auditors to whose number he belonged, but even by the elect. The latter no longer sought to hold things back from him, as in earlier days. He therefore learned many things about them he did not yet know. Later, he was to write a book about it entitled *De Moribus Manichaeorum* (The Way of Life of the Manichaeans).

This, too, was part of what we have called Augustine's novitiate. He obtained compelling proof that many of the "saints" of the sect known as the elect were saints in externals only. In actual fact, under their facade of Pharisaism they lived in a state of infernal decadence.

Thus everything combined to disappoint and disgust him. He already doubted God's word, and now he began to doubt men. This proved to be a great trial of heart and mind. The Academics taught that the truth is beyond the grasp of the human mind. Experience now seemed to show that virtuous living was equally beyond man's capacity. In the face of these new discouragements, Augustine felt he had to start all over again in his search for holiness and truth. Once he had rediscovered his "identity," as we would say nowadays, he would find the way to God and remain firmly on it until death.

At this moment of spiritual upheaval, Augustine received news that gave him some ray of hope. He learned that the chair of rhetoric in the city of Milan was vacant and the prefect of Rome, the famous Symmacus, who was still a pagan, had been asked to find someone to fill the post. This was a good omen for Augustine. If he obtained this position, his financial security was assured. He would become a public official in the employ of the city of Milan. At the same time, he could continue to have his own private students just as he had done in Carthage and Rome.

So Augustine looked around for someone to recommend him to Symmacus. The Manichaeans were willing to do this. As a pagan, Symmacus might have tended to reject any advances on the part of Catholics. In any event, Augustine tells us that his Manichaean friends intervened in his favor. Since he actually had the qualifications demanded for the post and found favor with Symmacus, he obtained the position he wanted so much.

Augustine had reached another turning point in his life, although he didn't realize it. In Milan he was destined to find the man appointed by God to lead him to the port of salvation.

8

Augustine Learns from Ambrose

Augustine and Ambrose

Saint Ambrose, bishop of Milan, was the man destined by God to bring Augustine back into the Church and prepare him to become one of her brightest lights.

At this point in his *Confessions*, Augustine writes:

"So I came to Milan, to the bishop and devout servant of God, Ambrose, famed among the best men of the whole world, whose eloquence did then most powerfully minister to *Your people the fatness of Your wheat and the joy of Your oil and the sober intoxication of Your wine.* All unknowing I was brought by God to him, that knowing I should be brought by him to God. That man of God received me as a father, and as bishop welcomed my coming. I came to love him, not at first

104

as a teacher of the truth, which I had utterly despaired of finding in Your Church, but for his kindness to me" (Book Five, XIII, p. 100).

Who was this man Ambrose? He was a Roman, probably born in the year 334 and who died on April 4th, 397. When Augustine came to Milan in the fall of 384, Ambrose was about fifty years old. Although born of Christian parents, he had not been baptized at birth. He was the son of a high Roman official, who died when he was very young. So, like Augustine, Ambrose was raised by his mother. He had a sister Marcellina who is honored as a saint, and also a brother Satyrus, likewise included in the roster of the saints.

Ambrose was the youngest of his family, and he entered a public career early in life. He became a member of the council of the prefect of the praetorium, Sextus Patronius Probus. In 370 Probus appointed Ambrose as *consularis*, that is to say, governor of the provinces of Liguria and Emilia, with an official residence in Milan.

The city of Milan was then greatly disturbed by the dissensions between Catholics and Arians. Ambrose had an arduous task maintaining the peace in the city. The story has often been told that when the Arian bishop, Auxentius, died in Milan, Ambrose gave such an eloquent panegyric that a child suddenly cried out: *"Ambrose, bishop!"* Whereupon the entire people made a show of hands voting him in as bishop. But this is now considered merely a legend, as it was by his earliest biographer Paulinus.

What is certain is that Ambrose was indeed asked to become bishop of Milan, and that he at first refused, objecting that he was not yet even baptized. Although he was over thirty years old, he was still only a catechumen. Besides, he was an official of the Empire. Only the Emperor could decide. At that time the Roman Emperor was Valentinian I, and he seemed flattered that one of his governors was deemed worthy to be a bishop. And so Ambrose agreed. Within the space of a week he received the sacraments of baptism, confirmation, and ordination. From that moment, he became a transformed man. He gave evidence of the loftiest piety, delved into the Scriptures, and exerted an ever-increasing influence on his flock. He had been a bishop exactly ten years (since December 7th, 374) when Augustine presented himself to him in the year 384.

At the feet of Ambrose

Augustine did not merely pay a courtesy call upon the bishop of Milan, in his new role as official rhetorician of the city. He was really eager to hear this renowned churchman preach, for he realized an orator always needs further training. So it was especially out of a professional man's curiosity that Monica's son hastened to the church where Ambrose was preaching. His dispositions were far removed from those of a potential convert to the Faith, as he himself has related:

"I attended carefully when he preached to the people, not with the right intention, but only to judge whether his eloquence was equal to his fame or whether it flowed higher or lower than had been told me. His words I listened to with the greatest care; his matter I held quite unworthy of attention" (*Confessions*, Book Five, XIII, p. 100).

Why such scorn on Augustine's part? Because he was still convinced Catholic doctrine could never satisfy him. He had already made up his mind to this after his futile efforts to study the Scriptures. He had found the Biblical style childish and plain, as compared with the ornate Ciceronian style he admired. Besides, the substance of the Scriptures had been vilified at the Manichaean meetings he had attended. As far as he was concerned, the Bible had nothing to offer.

However, as he continued to listen to Bishop Ambrose' sermons, an imperceptible change began to occur in his thinking. Although he was sure he would never change his mind, gradually his prejudices began to wane. We should not forget that sermons then consisted primarily of homilies on Holy Scripture. So Ambrose spoke about the Old and the New Testaments. He expounded, explained, and commented.

We should point out that from his study of Origen's writings Ambrose had acquired the tendency to stress the spiritual sense of the Biblical texts rather than their literal meaning. But even this was enlightening to Augustine. Without addressing himself specifically to the Manichaeans' clumsy criticisms of the Old Testament, Ambrose presented arguments that easily demolished them.

Augustine has testified in his *Confessions:* "Thus I did not take great heed to learn what he was saying but only to hear how he said it: that empty interest was all I now had since I despaired of man's finding the way to You. Yet along with the words, which I admired, there also came into my mind the subject-matter, to which I attached no importance. I could not separate them. And while I was opening my heart to learn how eloquently he spoke, I came to feel, though only gradually, how truly he spoke" (*Confessions*, Book Five, XIV, p. 100).

The first glimmers of light were beginning to penetrate Augustine's soul. However, Ambrose' teaching was not an organized course in Christian theology, for there was no such thing at that time. Teaching consisted primarily in reading and explaining the sacred books of Scripture, dealing now with one point of doctrine and then with another.

The first fruit of Ambrose' preaching for Augustine was to make him realize that Catholic doctrine was plausible and could hold the attention of an intelligent man. And yet this was the same religion as Monica's, the religion Augustine had learned from her as a young child. It could not, therefore, be just an old wives' tale.

"First I began to realize that there was a case for the things themselves, and I began to see that the Catholic Faith, for which I had thought nothing could be said in the face of the Manichaean objections, could be maintained on reasonable grounds: this especially after I had heard explained figuratively several passages of the Old Testament which had been a cause of death for me when taken literally" (*Confessions*, Book Five, XIV, pp. 100-101).

This was a giant step forward. But only one step. Augustine still had a long way to go. He later described his state of mind at that time as one of preparation. Monica's prayers and tears had won the first graces for him, without his realizing it. Let us quote him again:

"I did not yet know that [the Catholic Church] was teaching the truth, but I had found that she did not teach the things of which I had so strongly accused her. So I was first confounded and then enlightened. And I rejoiced, O my God, that Your only Church, the Body of Your only Son, in which the name of Christ had been put upon me while I was still an infant, had no taste for such puerile nonsense..." (*Confessions*, Book Six, IV, pp. 109-110).

The Manichaeans mocked the Church above all for representing God in human form in the accounts of the Old Testament, and comparing His wrath to that of an angry man. In his sermons Ambrose quietly explained that these were just popular ways of speaking, suited to our limited understanding. But, he pointed out, God is infinitely above our conceptions of Him and even beyond our capacity to express in words. Augustine wondered why he had not thought of that himself.

"...I was filled with shame — but joyful too — that I had been barking all these years not against the Catholic Faith but against mere figments of carnal imaginings" (*Confessions*, Book Six, III, p. 109).

Augustine has recalled at length the thoughts that came to his mind as he listened to Ambrose and the conclusions he reached:

"I determined, then, to go on as a catechumen in the Catholic Church — the Church of my parents — and to remain in that state until some certain light should appear by which I might steer my course" (*Confessions*, Book Five, XIV, p. 101).

And so Augustine was back to his starting point before he had joined the Manichaean sect. The title of catechumen had no great significance. For Augustine it involved no commitment at the time or even for the immediate future. There were many others like him in the Roman Empire of that day who sympathized with the Catholic Church but kept putting off their baptism until they were in danger of death.

Augustine knew that a catechumen duly registered in the Church's records over which Ambrose presided had the right to attend the first part of the liturgy which concluded with the bishop's homily. Before the Offertory, the *Missa* — or dismissal — of the catechumens was announced, for they were not permitted to participate in the sacred mysteries. There was also a second *Missa* or dismissal at the end of Mass, which was expressed in the words we still use today: *Ite, missa est* — "Go in peace to love and serve the Lord." It is from this command that the liturgy came to be known as the Mass.

Augustine was not yet interested in the sacred liturgy for its own sake. But the sermon was beginning to mean more and more to him. We can therefore understand his decision to remain a catechumen. He had reached this stage in his spiritual life when his mother arrived in Milan.

Monica in Milan

After Augustine left her disconsolate on the shores of North Africa, Monica had returned to Tagaste, sadly but with unimpaired trust in God. It is certain that her fugitive son sent word to her from Rome and later from Milan, since she ultimately joined him in Italy. Augustine continued to feel the effect of her prayers, especially when he was critically ill in Rome. He attributed his recovery solely to his mother's intercession.

Quite probably Augustine did not invite his mother to come to Milan. While he loved and respected her, he felt she encroached on his freedom. However he did let her know of his appointment as official rhetorician of the city of Milan. He wanted her to know that his future was now assured. Monica, for her part, yearned to be with him again, and to watch more closely over his spiritual welfare.

So Monica decided to leave Tagaste. It was no small task to settle her affairs and to set aside the money needed for the journey, but in the end she managed to do it. She probably sailed from Carthage in the year 385, overjoyed at the prospect of being reunited with this "son of many tears." A burning faith sustained her, as soon became apparent when the ship put out to sea. A terrible storm arose as the coast of Africa receded in the distance. Even the sailors thought the situation was hopeless. As Monica told Augustine later on, she was the only one aboard who was not afraid. It seemed unthinkable to her that God would deprive her of seeing her son again, especially as she had still so much to accomplish for him.

Above all else, Monica didn't want to die until her son had become a Catholic. God would certainly not refuse her this favor. Hadn't a holy bishop once told her so? And that is why she was the only serene person on the ship during the storm. She reassured the sailors by telling them that in a vision she had seen the ship reach port safely. That sufficed to restore everyone's courage. Soon her vision was fulfilled. The wind fell, the sea grew calm, and the journey proceeded without further incident.

The reunion

Monica finally arrived in Milan and was reunited with her son. After embracing her, Augustine hastened to tell her of his religious progress, since he knew this was what concerned her most. He thought she would be delighted to hear he was no longer a Manichaean and had become a catechumen once more. Contrary to his expectations, she showed neither surprise nor great joy. For Augustine to cease being a Manichaean was only a beginning.

Monica wanted her son to become a full-fledged Catholic, a fervent and obedient son of the Church. She wanted him to give up his irregular life and enter into an honorable marriage. We have many reasons to believe this was the sum of her ambitions for him. She had no idea that even before she died he would reach far greater heights, breaking all ties with the world and turning to a life of contemplation.

How surprised Monica would have been if she could have foreseen that her son Augustine was to go far higher still, and become one of the great bishops and doctors of the Church. She would have been even more thankful for all the tears he had cost her. But she had no idea how generously God would answer her prayers after seeming for so long not to hear them.

Without a moment's delay she told Augustine she was sure she would see him completely converted to the true Faith before she died. Augustine, of course, still held such an eventuality in serious doubt, and probably told her so. But his mother held fast to her now unshakable conviction.

Monica and Ambrose

The first thing Monica did after greeting her son and hearing his disclosures was to go and see Bishop Ambrose of Milan. From what Augustine had already told her, she was beginning to think of him as "an angel of God," to quote from the *Confessions*. She could hardly wait to talk with him, and ask what he thought of her son. She wanted to tell him how much she yearned for Augustine's conversion and beg him to pray for this intention. We know from Augustine's account that Ambrose was a very busy man, who kept his conversations very short and to the point. And yet he showed no impatience at Monica's confidences.

We are assured that Ambrose received Monica graciously and seemed to delight in looking at this mother whose love of God was readily discernible in her face. He listened to Monica as she told him how much her son had been impressed by his sermons, and of the hopes she held for his future. Monica, for her part, was drawn to the good bishop by his gentleness, kindness, and knowledge, and above all by his modesty. From that time on she always held him in highest veneration.

After this memorable encounter we might have expected rapid progress in Augustine's conversion. Now that Ambrose had been approached by this holy woman and apprized of her son's spiritual dispositions, would he not take the belated catechumen under his wing? Would he not ask him to come for instructions and thus hasten his acceptance into the Church? Not at all.

Ambrose was a man who counted above all on God's grace and not on his own capacities. In his opinion, it was best to let things take their course. Like the great Saint Vincent de Paul in seventeenth-century France, he practiced the motto: "Never trespass upon Providence."

Ambrose made no overtures. Did he expect Augustine to come and talk to him of his own accord? Perhaps, but he offered him no opportunity to do so. He didn't even seem to notice Augustine's desire to talk with him. He had greater faith in Monica's prayers than in his own exhortations. In any event, Augustine has written a famous passage on this matter. According to the *Confessions:*

"[Ambrose did not] know how I was inflamed nor the depth of my peril. I could not ask of him what I wished as I wished, for I was kept from any face-to-face conversation with him by the throng of men with their own troubles, whose infirmities he served. The very little time he was not with these he was, refreshing either his body with necessary food or his mind with reading" *(Confessions,* Book Six, III, p. 108).

Augustine often came to see Ambrose in his free time, usually during the afternoon. But what transpired?

The *Confessions* tell us:

"No one was forbidden to approach him, nor was it his custom to require that visitors should be announced: but when we came to him we often saw him reading and always to himself; and after we had sat long in silence, unwilling to interrupt a work on which he was so intent, we would depart again. We guessed that in the small time he could find for the refreshment of his mind, he would wish to be free from the distraction of other men's affairs and not called away from what he was doing. Perhaps he was on his guard lest [if he read aloud] someone listening should be troubled and want an explanation if the author he was reading expressed some idea over obscurely, and it might be necessary to expound or discuss some of the more difficult questions. And if he had to spend time on this, he would get through less reading than he wished. Or it may be that his real reason for reading to himself was to preserve his voice, which did in fact readily grow tired. But whatever his reason for doing it, that man certainly had a good reason" (Book Six, III, p. 108).

Neither Augustine nor Monica resented Ambrose's reserve. They had too much respect for him for that. But this did not advance Augustine's conversion. He concludes:

"Anyhow I was given no opportunity of putting such questions as I desired to that holy oracle of Yours, unless they were of a sort to be heard briefly. But the agitation working in me required that he should be fully at leisure if I were to pour it out before him; and I never found him so" (*Confessions*, Book Six, III, p. 108).

So the young orator, then thirty-one, kept haunting the study of the bishop twenty years his senior, in the hope of opening his soul to him. Always he found Ambrose so busy, burdened by pastoral problems, engrossed in reading for his recreation as well as the needs of his ministry, that he dared not disturb him. Augustine had so many things on his mind that it would have taken many hours to recite the litany of his spiritual concerns. He was well aware Ambrose did not have time to hear him out.

This is not to imply that Ambrose was blind to Augustine's tactics. To his mind, God has an hour for everything, and Augustine's hour would finally come. In the end, Ambrose had the joy of baptizing Augustine at the time decreed by God, although Monica's prayers hastened that long-awaited day.

Monica's obedience

For all her impatience, Monica never for an instant thought of accusing Ambrose of indifference. She was deeply devoted to the holy bishop, and Augustine has related a little incident in proof of it.

In Africa it was the custom to celebrate the feasts of the martyrs by going to the shrines where they were entombed. Offerings of bread, cakes, and wine were brought in a basket and placed for a moment on the tomb. Then a portion of the food was given to the poor, and the donors took the remainder home to eat at a family gathering. This practice did lead to abuses. Some Africans used to take advantage of the honor rendered to their martyrs to eat and drink more than usual. Naturally this posed no danger for Monica. But those inclined to eat and drink too much could claim they were doing so as an act of devotion.

Ambrose had banned the custom in Milan both because of the abuses to which it could lead and because he felt it was too reminiscent of the *parentalia*[1] festivities celebrated by the pagans.

Monica was not aware of this prohibition. On one occasion she arrived at a shrine to celebrate the feast of a martyr, and was dumbfounded when the sacristan refused to let her enter, saying that Bishop Ambrose condemned this practice. At that period of history, we might point out that the sacristan, although a married man, was ordained and hence a member of the clergy. Monica not only hastened to obey him, but did not even exhibit the slightest sign of displeasure. Augustine relates:

"When she found that the custom was forbidden...she abandoned the practice quite willingly. In place of her basket filled with the fruits of the earth, she learned to offer at the shrines of the martyrs a breast full of prayers purer than any such gifts. Thus she was able to give what she could to the needy; and the Communion of the Lord's Body was celebrated where the martyrs had been immolated and crowned in the likeness of His passion" (*Confessions*, Book Six, II, pp. 106-107).

1. This was the chief annual festival of the dead in ancient Rome, celebrated between February 13 and 21.

Augustine comments on the incident in a witty manner:

"But yet, O Lord my God, it does seem to me — and upon this matter my heart is in Your sight — that my mother might not so easily have borne the breaking of her custom if it had been forbidden by some other whom she did not love as she loved Ambrose. For on account of my salvation she loved him dearly; and he loved her on account of her most religious way of life, for she was fervent in spirit and ever doing good, for she haunted the church. So that when he saw me he often broke out in her praises, congratulating me that I had such a mother, and not realizing what sort of a son she had: for I doubted all these things and did not believe that the way of life could be discovered" (*Confessions*, Book Six, II, p. 107).

The example we have cited shows there were minor differences of ritual among the various Christian Churches. Another example can be found in the matter of fasting. In Africa, Saturday was a fast day. But Monica was told this was not the rule in Milan. She wondered whether or not she should follow the custom of Tagaste. Shrewdly seizing an opportunity to have Augustine see Ambrose, she sent him to the holy bishop for a definitive answer on the question of fasting. Ambrose, with great courtesy but briefly as usual, answered: "Follow the custom of the Church where you are. If you are in Rome, fast with the Church of Rome. But if you are in Milan, do not fast, because the Church of Milan does not fast."

As we shall see in the next chapter, Augustine was to receive guidance and instruction from one of Ambrose's great friends, although he had been hoping to be taught by the Bishop of Milan himself.

9

The Homestretch

A mother's efforts

We know nothing about Monica's conversations with the holy bishop of Milan, short and furtive as they were. And yet he must have made her understand, if only by a word or two, that it was not enough for her son to accept the Christian faith intellectually in order to be baptized. He also had to live according to Christian moral principles. As we know, Augustine had been living with a mistress, and their illegitimate son was now fourteen or fifteen years old. But it seems Augustine never seriously considered marrying the mother of his son.

We have no idea what the obstacle was to such a marriage, but we can surmise several canonical impediments to it. For example, Augustine's companion may have been a baptized Christian, married to a Christian and perhaps abandoned

by him. If such were the case, it was absolutely impossible for Augustine to make this woman his
legitimate wife.

Whether this was the obstacle or something else,
it is certain Monica determined to get her son into
a matrimonial situation acceptable to the Church. For
by now Augustine's intellectual objections against
receiving baptism had all but disappeared.

Indeed, it was perhaps because of Augustine's
marital problem that Ambrose had been reluctant to
listen to his intellectual difficulties. Monica could
understand this, and so she set to work to remove the
obstacle. Preparation of mind is a fine thing, but
preparation of heart and conscience is far more important.

It would take all of Monica's initiative to find a
suitable solution. For one thing, Augustine was not a
man inclined to the celibate life. As he himself has
declared in his *Confessions*, he admired and envied
everything about Ambrose *except his celibacy*.

Monica therefore set out to do two things. First,
she must find Augustine a worthy wife. In the second
place, she had to separate him from the companion
with whom he had lived for many years. These were
arduous tasks. In her need, Monica turned as usual
to prayer. This time she quickly obtained everything
she sought.

Perhaps with Bishop Ambrose' help, Monica
found a young girl in a Christian family of Milan
suitable to become Augustine's wife. Augustine
finally agreed to her plan, although he was deeply
attached to his companion. Once Monica had obtained
his consent, the marriage was decided upon. However, the girl was still very young. Besides, a proper
period of time had to elapse between the breaking of
Augustine's liaison and any legitimate marriage. It
was therefore decided to wait two years.

Everything was proceeding smoothly up to that
point. There was, however, another hurdle to sur-

mount. Augustine's mistress, whose name has not come down to us, had to be persuaded to accept the separation. She was, of course, the mother of Adeodatus, Augustine's son.

For all her mistakes, this woman proved herself far above the common run. Despite her tears and her great reluctance to give up her lover and son, she had the courage to agree to the separation out of love for Augustine and for the sake of his eternal salvation. Far more edifying still is the fact that she decided to enter a monastery to atone for her sins. Augustine wrote of her:

"My heart, which had held her very dear, was broken and wounded and shed blood. She went back to Africa, swearing that she would never know another man, and left with me the natural son I had had of her. But I in my unhappiness could not, for all my manhood, imitate her resolve" (*Confessions*, Book Six, XV, p. 126).

Yes, Augustine had overestimated his strength. He was still too much of an intellectual and did not yet know man's need of constant prayer. In time, he would freely embrace celibacy and persevere in it until death. But when he first tried to practice it after his mistress left him, he found it unbearable. He has sadly and humbly admitted it in his *Confessions:*

"I was unable to bear the delay of two years which must pass before I was to get the girl I had asked for in marriage. In fact it was not really marriage that I wanted. I was simply a slave to lust. So I took another woman, not of course as a wife; and thus my soul's disease was nourished and kept alive vigorously as ever, indeed worse than ever.... Nor was the wound healed that had been made by the cutting off of my former mistress. For there was first burning and bitter grief; and after that it festered, and as the pain grew duller it only grew more hopeless" (Book Six, XV, p. 126).

What shame and sorrow for Monica! Were her plans going to crumble after all? Had all her efforts and prayers been in vain?

Monica knew the state of Augustine's soul, for he sometimes talked to her about it. She also knew of his new liaison. He was then surrounded by admirers and friends, including his inseparable Alypius, and Nebridius, a young fellow-African from Tagaste. He had admitted in their presence that he was ready to rank Epicurus above all other philosophers. In other words, he was coming to think that pleasure is all that matters in a man's life, and that outside of pleasure there is nothing. To quote him:

"And I put the question, supposing we were immortals and could live in perpetual enjoyment of the body without any fear of loss, why we should not then be happy, or what else should we seek" (*Confessions*, Book Six, XVI, p. 127).

When such words were reported to Monica, she may well have envisioned the shipwreck of all her hopes. However, she persevered in her plans with admirable courage.

At that period of Augustine's life, the only barrier to disaster for him consisted in the training he had received from his mother as a child.

"I became more wretched and You more close to me. Your right hand was ready to pluck me from the mire and wash me clean, though I knew it not. So far nothing called me back from the depth of the gulf of carnal pleasure save fear of death and of the judgment to come, which, through all the fluctuations of my opinions, never left my mind" (Book Six, XVI, p. 127).

Here we have a striking example of the efficacy of the Christian teachings on death and judgment. While true religion develops in an ambience of love, the fact remains that fear of divine justice can serve as a brake against the onslaughts of the devil in hours of darkness and peril.

Augustine was suffering bitterly from his fruitless searches and disappointments:

"What were the agonies, what the anguish of my heart in labor, O my God! But though I knew it not, You were listening.... You knew what I was suffering and no man knew it. For how little it was that my tongue uttered of it in the ears even of my closest friends! Could they hear the tumult of my soul?... Yet into Your hearing came all that I cried forth in the anguish of my heart" (*Confessions*, Book Seven, VII, p. 141).

The books of the Platonists

As had so often happened before, help came to Augustine from the most unexpected source. At this moment of his life he came across some of Plato's works translated by a well-known Roman rhetorician recently converted to Christianity. This man's name was Victorinus.

Augustine devoured the books, as he usually did when he made literary discoveries. He was fascinated by the thought of this greatest of Greek philosophers. Plato had reached up beyond all material things, professed the loftiest idealism, ranked ideas above matter, and explained all things perceptible to the senses in the light of God's eternal Ideas. Plato's works even glimpsed the doctrine of the Word, which holds such a high place in the Christian faith. Until then Augustine had known nothing of Plato except perhaps that he was a famous man mentioned by Cicero. But let us see how the reading of Plato started a revolution in his mind:

"About that time, a book came into my hands filled, to use the words of an ancient writer, with the most excellent attars of Arabia. As soon as I began to breathe in its fragrance, as soon as a few drops of it fell on the tiny flame that was beginning to burn in my heart, it is impossible to understand what a great conflagration suddenly erupted within me. It is impossible for you, Romanianus; impossible for me. Now neither honors, nor human pomps, nor desires for glory, nor the charms and enticements of this earthly life—indeed, nothing touched me anymore, in the presence of the light I was beginning to glimpse!"

Augustine once more reveals himself to be a man of sensibility, open to the things of the spirit and secretly yearning to be liberated from the carnal passions that were consuming him. At the age of thirty-two he was set afire by reading Plato, just as he had been by Cicero's *Hortensius* when he was nineteen.

The problem was still the same: the superiority of the soul over the body, of the spiritual life over the carnal. But now there was an added element. In reading Plato Augustine was amazed to discover the thought of St. John the Evangelist. That a great pagan philosopher should present the theory of the Word seemed to confirm the doctrine of the Word in the teaching of the Catholic Church. In short, he was reading Plato, but he could not help doing so in the light of his childhood's faith, the faith of his mother and of the great Bishop Ambrose.

However it was soon apparent to him that Plato, for all his genius, had not reached the heights of St. John. It was impossible to find anywhere in Plato the magnificent thought that had become the faith of Christians: *"The Word became flesh and made his dwelling among us"* (John 1:14).

Plato had known nothing of the great themes of the Gospel: the fall of man through sin, God's mercy, the Incarnation of the Word, the redemptive death of Christ on the cross. Evidently Augustine did not at first understand all these things, but he has said that he kept hearing a voice crying out to him:

"Courage! I am the food of the strong. And you will eat me. But it is not I who shall be changed into

you, for you shall be changed into me!" (*Confessions,*
Book Seven, X)

He truly heard these words, not in his intellect
but in his heart. He goes on to say:

"There was from that moment no ground of
doubt in me: I would more easily have doubted my
own life than have doubted that truth is: which is
clearly seen, being understood by the things that are
made" (*Confessions,* Book Seven, X, p. 145).

Above all, Plato taught Augustine the meaning
of the word *spirit.* Until then, and especially during
his Manichaean period, he had been unable to form
a correct idea of God because he had no idea what a
pure spirit was. With the help of Plato he was now
able to distinguish spirit from matter and all material
things. Through Plato, likewise, he began to grasp
the depth of Christian doctrine. He came to see that
although the Scriptures were written in such a simple
and unpretentious style that the most uneducated
person could understand them, they contained profound teachings to delight and nourish even the most
brilliant minds.

Augustine and St. Paul

Monica rejoiced to see her son turn to more
noble thoughts. As we know, Augustine was always
eager to share his enthusiasms with others. Now he
talked of Plato with Alypius, Nebridius, and other
disciples close to him. He also talked about these
things to his mother, who saw signs of spiritual
progress in her son. She must have seen he was
now ready to be nourished by the Epistles of St. Paul.

While St. John speaks of the Word in a sublime
manner, St. Paul describes the willful abasements
of the Son of God in unforgettable accents. He lays
bare man's inner conflicts, the root of the tragic
dualism within each of us which the Manichaeans
explained by false arguments. In St. Paul's writings

the whole mystery of the human drama unfolded before Augustine's mind. He realized the infinite distance that exists between the most sublime discoveries of the philosophers and the teachings of divine revelation transmitted by God's envoys whom we call the apostles.

No one has ever spoken as Paul did, or revealed man so clearly to himself as he does in his Epistles. We have only to recall a passage such as this:

"What happens is that I do, not the good I will to do, but the evil I do not intend.... This means that even though I want to do what is right, a law that leads to wrongdoing is always ready at hand.... What a wretched man I am! Who can free me from this body under the power of death? All praise to God, through Jesus Christ our Lord!" (Romans 7:19-25)

It is God's grace that saves man. Some day Augustine, following in the footsteps of Paul, would proclaim its mysteries, its necessity, its action within us, and its fruits of salvation and joy. From his very first contact with St. Paul, he was filled with enthusiasm for his writings:

"So now I seized greedily upon the adorable writing of Your Spirit, and especially upon the Apostle Paul.... In that pure eloquence I...found that whatever truth I had read in the Platonists was said here with praise of Your grace: that he who sees should *not so glory as if he had not received*—and received, indeed, not only what he sees but even the power to see, *for what has he that he has not received?* And further, that he [who sees] is not only taught to see You who are always the same, but is also strengthened to take hold of You.... For though a man be delighted with the law of God according to the inward man, what shall he do about that other law in his members, fighting against the law of his mind and captivating him in the law of sin that is in his members? ...But what shall unhappy man do? *Who shall deliver him from the body of this death, save the grace of God by Jesus Christ our Lord...in whom the prince of this world found nothing worthy of death yet killed Him; and the handwriting was blotted out of the decree which was contrary to us.*

"The writings of the Platonists contain nothing of all this. Their pages show nothing of the face of that love, the tears of confession, Your sacrifice, an afflicted spirit, a contrite and humbled heart, the salvation of Your people, the espoused city, the promise of the Holy Spirit, the chalice of our redemption" *(Confessions,* Book Seven, XXI, pp. 153-154).

All these truths, absent from the books of the philosophers, explained Augustine to himself, speaking to him of his own struggles, disappointments, efforts and failures. But here they were in St. Paul. Augustine would never forget it. The last mists of doubt and error were clearing away from his mind. He would still need to make a decisive leap forward, to find encouragement and a contagion of sorts from those around him. He was finally convinced, but he was afraid. He mistrusted himself and his strength. He realized a battle was raging within him, and he knew whence it came. He also knew what he had to do to come out the victor. But he was not yet willing to humble himself, join in his mother's tears, throw himself at the feet of his God, repent of his sins and overcome his passions.

Monica saw what was going on in her son, even guessing the things he did not tell her. She did all in her power to help him. For one thing, she seems to have been successful in quickly breaking up the liaison he had formed after sending Adeodatus' mother away. But he still had to realize how inferior he was to so many valiant Christians far less educated than he but immeasurably more courageous in the practice of the virtues. At this juncture God chose to offer him examples of Christian living that would spur him on by making him realize his own cowardice compared with the vigorous efforts of the simplest believers. As yet he did not even suspect what greatness lay within their souls.

At the home of Simplicianus

Augustine continued to be tormented, divided against himself, urged on by his mother and harassed by his own conscience. Perhaps at the suggestion of Ambrose, who was now busier and more inaccessible than ever, he finally decided to consult a holy priest of Milan named Simplicianus.

Simplicianus was a venerable old man, with a wide experience of human nature and life. It was he who had baptized Ambrose, after giving him instructions. Augustine came to him with the desires, fears, difficulties and weaknesses that still held him back. The aged priest took care not to reprimand him in any way or show the slightest surprise at all the things Augustine told him. For what was happening to the young seeker was the common fate of all the children of Adam and Eve.

Simplicianus talked most about Victorinus, the Roman rhetorician whose translations of Plato he had read. As it happened, he had known Victorinus well, for the latter had come to him during his early search for the Christian faith. Like Augustine, Victorinus was attracted to Christianity, but hesitated to make a firm commitment to it. He saw no urgent need for such a step.

Speaking in confidence, Victorinus once said to Simplicianus: "Do you realize that I am a Christian?" Simplicianus answered: "I shall believe it only when I see you in the Church of Christ!" Victorinus retorted: "Why? Is it walls that make a Christian?"

What really held Victorinus back was human respect. He was well-known, a man with friends and admirers among both pagans and Christians.

He didn't want to jeopardize his reputation. It had already earned him a statue in the forum. But he continued to read, reflect, and pray. One day he finally made up his mind to place greater value on the approval of Jesus Christ than on that cf men. Going to his friend Simplicianus, he said: "Let us go to the church, so that I can become a Christian!"

The conversion of a man like Victorinus caused a sensation in Rome. That had been twenty years earlier. Victorinus had handled the matter well. When the moment came for him and the other catechumens to make their profession of faith, he was advised to make his secretly so as not to be ridiculous in the eyes of the crowds. But he energetically refused to make a secret of his faith. Proudly standing up before everyone he *"rendered the Creed,"* as the saying of the time was, making his profession of faith before everyone. And he was a man whose name was whispered ecstatically everywhere he went. "There goes Victorinus!"

The entire Church of Rome was consoled by this fine example. Afterward, Victorinus gloried only in being a humble child in the footsteps of Christ. When Julian the Apostate prohibited Christians from teaching literature, Victorinus retired from his profession and spent the rest of his life in silence and meditation.

The example of Victorinus made a profound impression on Augustine. Here was one of his own colleagues, a man older than he, recognized by all for his superior talent. Augustine could not help admiring his courage. Even though his passions churned madly within him, he could still open his mind to spiritual enthusiasms. He had the capacity to admire true worth. When he thought of Victorinus, his heart yearned to imitate him. And so he left Simplicianus in a sort of ecstasy.

"Come, Lord, work upon us, call us back, set us on fire and clasp us close, be fragrant to us, draw us

to Your loveliness: let us love, let us run to You"
(*Confessions*, Book Eight, IV, p. 163).

But deep within his soul the battle continued to
rage. As he has admitted many times, he kept whisper-
ing: "Lord, heal me, but not yet! Soon, but give me
just a little while." He was answering "Yes!" to God's
grace, but many dark forces within him kept saying
"No!"

In his *Confessions*, he relates:

"Now, O Lord, my Helper and my Redeemer, I
shall tell and confess to Your name how You delivered
me from the chain of that desire of the flesh which
held me so bound, and from the servitude of worldly
things. I went my usual way with a mind ever more
anxious, and day after day I sighed for You" (Book
Eight, VI, p. 166).

And yet his new will was not strong enough to
overcome his old self, entrenched in evil habits. Thus
as he said, he had two wills, one old and the other
new, one carnal and the other spiritual. And these
two wills fought a deadly battle within his soul.

Augustine remained hesitant and undecided. He
was, as he put it, like a sleeping man who knows he
must get up but resists semiconsciously, muttering:
"In a little while, yes, in a little while, in just a
moment!"

Monica was naturally disappointed by her son's
dalliance, especially after the hopes he had given her
at the time of his visit to Simplicianus. She began to
fear she would never attain her goal, but soon re-
gained heart and resumed her prayers. She would
not rest until she had obtained her beloved son's
conversion.

The heroism of Ambrose

Milan was then in the throes of serious unrest.
Ambrose's firm action in combating the Church's
peril had its influence on Augustine. For it offered

him a chance to see what a man can accomplish when his natural courage has been increased tenfold through the grace of faith.

Empress Justine had once belonged to the Arian sect. As regent during the minority of her son, Emperor Valentinian II, she dared ask Ambrose to turn over to the Arians a church used by the Catholics of Milan, either the cathedral church of Ambrose or the Portiana basilica. Ambrose flatly refused to obey the empress' command, stating that it was not proper for a bishop to turn a temple of the Lord over to heretics.

Needless to say, the all-powerful regent-mother was furious. She sent out a detachment of soldiers to seize the Portiana basilica. Ambrose's cathedral was also surrounded. But the Catholic faithful were indignant and confronted the soldiers near the cathedral. The soldiers withdrew to the Portiana basilica. A civil war of sorts had broken out in the city.

Meanwhile, Ambrose did not leave his church. He kept talking to his people, expressing the hope that blood would not flow in Milan and urging his people to persevere with him in prayer. The cathedral was constantly filled with faithful who wanted to protect their bishop. Ambrose stood in his pulpit in the rear of the choir, behind the altar, preaching to his people. He would read and explain the sacred Scriptures, recommend calm and respect for law. At the same time he praised fidelity to holy liberty of soul and to the Church, the mother of liberty.

When summons were brought to him in the name of the empress, Ambrose proudly answered the nobles and tribunes sent by Justine, saying:

"If the emperor demanded what belongs to me, even though everything I own belongs to the poor, I would not refuse. But the things of God are not mine. If anyone wants my patrimony, let him take it! If anyone wants my body, let him seize it! Do you want to put me in chains and lead me to death? I shall obey, and shall not allow my people to defend me. I shall not kiss the altars, begging for life. I prefer to be immolated on the altars!"

Calligone, prefect of the imperial chamber said to him: "You are being contemptuous of Valentinian, and for that I shall have your head!" Ambrose simply answered: "God grant you may carry out your threat. I shall act as a bishop, and you as a eunuch."

Nothing could shake Ambrose's resolve. Several incidents occurred, but he remained invincible. The conflict was still going on at Eastertime of the year 386, and Ambrose remained in his cathedral without ever leaving it. The faithful stood firmly behind him. In those days Christian basilicas consisted of various areas. There were lateral rooms and annexes where it was possible to rest while remaining within the precincts of the church.

To keep his people busy, Ambrose had the genial idea of introducing a custom already established in the East. This was the chanting of the psalms by two alternating choirs, so as not to tire the singers. This custom has been perpetuated to the present time in the chanting of Vespers, as well as in the singing of the *Gloria* and the *Creed* in the Eucharistic liturgy.

Better still, Ambrose maintained such mastery over his mind and emotions during his church's siege that he was able to compose many Latin hymns. These he gave to his faithful to sing, and they complied with great enthusiasm. Many of these hymns have been used over the centuries in the Western liturgy. While Ambrose did not compose many of those attributed to him, historians agree that his most beautiful hymns have been preserved. Of course, he may well have composed some of them before the crisis of 386.

Monica in the forefront

We have gone into some detail about the Catholic-Arian conflict in Milan because we know from the *Confessions* that Monica was one of the most ardent followers of Ambrose to profess the true Faith against Arianism.

Monica would stand close to Ambrose's pulpit, listening to his every word and ready to obey his every command. She sang the psalms with her whole soul. She took very much to heart the anxieties and struggles of the Church. After her concern for her son's spiritual welfare came her desire to serve the holy bishop of Milan in his struggles for the Catholic Faith. Augustine was also deeply moved by the heroism he witnessed at that time. In this connection, he has written in his *Confessions:*

"I regarded Ambrose as a lucky man by worldly standards to be held in honor by such important people: only his celibacy seemed to me a heavy burden. I had no means of guessing, and no experience of my own to learn from, what hope he bore within him, what struggles he might have against the temptations that went with his high place, what was his consolation in adversity, and on what joys of Your bread the hidden mouth of his heart fed" (*Confessions,* Book Six, III, p. 107).

The day would come when Augustine finally understood all these things. Indeed, it was fast approaching.

10

Monica's Victory

The arrival of Ponticianus

Soon after Milan had returned to normal the denouement of Augustine's spiritual drama came about in a most unexpected way.

Ponticianus, one of Augustine's friends from Africa, came to visit him in Milan. They had known each other as youths. But whereas Augustine had abandoned the faith of his childhood, Ponticianus had steadfastly persevered in his religious beliefs. He was now a high-ranking military officer in the emperor's entourage.

This was probably not his first visit to Augustine. In every age compatriots tend to seek each other out when they are abroad, to reminisce about their native land. On that particular day, Ponticianus noticed a book on a gaming table in Augustine's home and opened it. He expected to see a work by Cicero or Quintilian in the home of his rhetorician friend. Instead, he found the *Epistles of Saint Paul.* Somewhat surprised, he looked at Augustine with a smile as if to ask him if he thought he would find examples of elegant literary style in it. Augustine admitted he found great charm in the writings of St. Paul. The conversation then became more intimate and turned to religious matters.

The hermits of the desert

Ponticianus had traveled extensively, for the Roman legions were sent all over the Empire. He had been in Gaul, Spain, Africa, Egypt, as well as in Italy. Soon he was telling Augustine about what he had seen, especially in Egypt. There were several desert regions in Egypt, including the Thebaid and Scete, among others. There Ponticianus had admired the hermits, men who had left the bustling centers of worldly activity to live in austere solitude and think only of God. For them the desert had become a paradise.

These were not just a few isolated groups. There were five thousand hermits on the mountain of Nitria alone. Farther away, at about a half-day's march, two thousand more lived in a place called Cella. Each hermit lived in a bare cell separated from all the others. They gathered only on Saturday to spend the Lord's day together in prayer and chanting. Elsewhere there were nearly ten thousand under the rule of a holy abbot named Serapion. There were almost as many hermits under the rule of St. Macarius. Finally, St. Pachomius had just died in the Thebaid, leaving more than seven thousand hermits. After his death so many monks adopted his rule that more than fifty thousand of them gathered for the General Congregation of Monasteries.

Strangely enough, Augustine had never heard anything about all this. He listened to Ponticianus' accounts with rapt interest, and never tired of hearing about the life of total consecration to the contemplation of God. Now everything he had discovered in *Hortensius* or even in the works of Plato seemed to pale into insignificance. To think these things had been going on during his own lifetime and he had known nothing about it!

The West was just beginning to talk about the great monastic movement in the East. The great Athanasius, Bishop of Alexandria, Egypt, had thought it worth his precious time to write the life of the greatest of these anchorites or hermits, St. Anthony of Egypt. When Athanasius was exiled for his faith far from his native land and sent to Treves in the wilderness of Gaul, he brought with him written accounts of these wonderful happenings.

It was now Ponticianus' turn to be surprised. Augustine was an admirer of Ambrose and never missed one of his sermons. And yet he did not know the good bishop had written some magnificent books in praise of *Holy Virginity*, that is to say, total consecration to God alone. Augustine has related:

"Alypius and I stood amazed to hear of Your wonderful works, done in the true faith and in the Catholic Church so recently, practically in our own times, and with such numbers of witnesses. All three of us were filled with wonder, we, because the deeds we were now hearing were so great, and he because we had never heard them before" (*Confessions*, Book Eight, VI, p. 167).

A striking example

Ponticianus never tired of talking about the monastic life, especially as he saw that Augustine and his inseparable companions were so deeply interested in it. Sensing the curiosity of his hearers, he gave the following account, which has been recorded for us by Augustine:

"He continued with his discourse and we listened in absolute silence. It chanced that he told how on one occasion he and three of his companions — it was at Treves, when the emperor was at the chariot races in the Circus — had gone one afternoon to walk in the gardens close by the city walls. As it happened they fell into two groups, one of the others staying with him, and the other two likewise walking their own way. But as those other two strolled on they came into a certain house, the dwelling of some servants of Yours, poor in spirit, of whom is the kingdom of God. There they found a small book in which was written the life of Anthony. One of them began to read it, marveled at it, was inflamed by it. While he was actually reading he had begun to think how he might embrace such a life, and give up his worldly employment to serve You alone. For the two men were both state officials.

"Suddenly the man who was doing the reading was filled with a love of holiness and angry at himself with righteous shame. He looked at his friend and said to him: 'Tell me, please, what is the goal of our ambition in all these labors of ours? What are we aiming at? What is our motive in being in the public service? Have we any higher hope at court than to be friends of the emperor? And at that level, is not everything uncertain and full of perils?... But if I should choose to be a friend of God, I can become one now.'

"He said this, and, all troubled with the pain of the new life coming to birth in him, he...read on and was changed inwardly, where You alone could see; and the world dropped away from his mind.... At length he broke out in heavy weeping, saw the better way and chose it for his own. Being now Your servant, he said to his friend, 'Now I have broken from that hope we had and have decided to serve God;

and I enter upon that service from this hour, in this place. If you have no will to imitate me, at least do not try to dissuade me.' The other replied that he would remain his companion in so great a service for so great a prize. So the two of them, now Your servants, built a spiritual tower at the only cost that is adequate, the cost of leaving all things and following You.

"Then Ponticianus and the man who had gone walking with him in another part of the garden came looking for them in the same place, and when they found them they suggested that they should return home as the day was now declining. But they told of their decision and their purpose, and how that will had arisen in them and was now settled in them; and asked them not to try to argue them out of their decision.... Ponticianus and his friend, though not changed from their former state, yet wept for themselves, as he told us, and congratulated them in God and commended themselves to their prayers.

"Then with their own hearts trailing in the dust they went off to the palace, while the other two, with their hearts fixed upon heaven, remained in the hut. But these men, as it happened, were betrothed, and when the two women heard of it they likewise dedicated their virginity to You" (*Confessions*, Book Eight, VI, pp. 167-169).

The storm breaks

Ponticianus was so engrossed in his story that he was totally unaware of the impression he was making on his hearers, especially Augustine. As long as he talked about the anchorites of the desert, Augustine listened with calm approval. When he came to the account of his fellow soldiers at Treves, Augustine listened more attentively. Then came the passage: "What are we aiming at? Have we no higher hopes than to be the emperor's friends? And what good will that do us? Why not become the friends of God!" These words loosed a veritable tornado in Augustine's heart. This was what he had been asking himself over and over: What is life all about? Why are we on this earth? And in what mire I have lived thus far! To quote again from the *Confessions:*

"This was the story Ponticianus told. But You, Lord, while he was speaking, turned me back towards myself.... And You set me there before my own face that I might see how vile I was, how twisted, and unclean and spotted and ulcerous. I saw myself and was horrified; but there was no way to flee from myself.... For many years had flowed by—a dozen or more—from the time when I was nineteen and was stirred by the reading of Cicero's *Hortensius* to the study of wisdom; and here was I still postponing the giving up of this world's happiness to devote myself to the search for that of which not the finding only but the mere seeking is better than to find all the treasures and kingdoms of men, better than all the body's pleasures....

"I had thought that my reason for putting off from day to day the following of You alone to the contempt of earthly hopes was that I did not see any certain goal towards which to direct my course. But now the day was come when I stood naked in my own sight and my conscience accused me: 'Why is my voice not heard? Surely you are the man who used to say that you could not cast off vanity's baggage for an uncertain truth. Very well: now the truth is certain, yet you are still carrying the load...'" (*Confessions,* Book Eight, VII, pp. 169-170).

As Ponticianus spoke, Augustine was overcome with remorse, shame, and disgust with himself. In a kind of mad rage, he tracked his passions down into the hidden recesses of his soul, and his face betrayed his inner turmoil.

In the garden

Ponticianus' visit was over. Augustine was too overcome by emotion to accompany him to the gate. Alypius went in his place. Meanwhile, Augustine withdrew into a quiet corner of the garden.

Monica had been present during the entire encounter. Her mother's intuition caught her son's reactions. But this was not the time to talk to him. In her heart she sensed that God's hour had at last come. And so she went her way, turning to prayer more intensely than ever before. Almost all the Augustinian liturgies have declared that Monica fell on her knees and prayed during her son's spiritual travail. Although he didn't suspect it, it was to be a real childbirth, by which he would be born to a new life.

When Alypius returned to Augustine, the latter shouted out to him in excitement:

"What is wrong with us? What is this that you heard? The unlearned arise and take heaven by force, and here we are with all our learning, stuck fast in flesh and blood! Is there any shame in following because they have gone before us; would it not be a worse shame not to follow at once?" (*Confessions*, Book Eight, VIII, p. 171)

Without waiting for an answer, Augustine felt himself being led still farther. Alypius kept looking at him in mute astonishment. For he had never seen his teacher Augustine the prey to such emotion. His voice, his flushed face, his words, all betrayed unbelievable excitement on his part.

Augustine kept hearing a voice within saying: "Let it be now! Let it be now!" And yet even in this decisive hour of his life the voices he knew all too well still tried to entice him.

"Those trifles of all trifles, and vanities of vanities, my one-time mistresses, held me back, plucking at my garment of flesh and murmuring softly:

'Are you sending us away?' And 'From this moment shall this or that not be allowed you, now or forever?' What were they suggesting to me in the phrase I have written 'this or that,' what were they suggesting to me, O my God? Do You in Your mercy keep from the soul of Your servant the vileness and uncleanness they were suggesting" (*Confessions,* Book Eight, XI, p. 176).

Soon these pleadings grew weaker until they were only confused murmurings within him. The voice of his past was not so clear and strong. Instead, he began to think of the great army of those who had consecrated themselves to the Lord about whom Ponticianus had been telling him. And Augustine said to himself:

"Can you not do what these men have done, what these women have done? Or could men or women have done such in themselves, and not in the Lord their God? The Lord their God gave me to them. Why do you stand upon yourself and so not stand at all? Cast yourself upon Him and be not afraid; He will not draw away and let you fall. Cast yourself without fear, He will receive you and heal you" (*Confessions,* Book Eight, XI, p. 177).

And he goes on:
"Yet I was still ashamed, for I could still hear the murmurings of those vanities, and I still hung hesitant.... This was the controversy raging in my heart, a controversy about myself against myself. And Alypius stayed by my side and awaited in silence the issue of such agitation as he had never seen in me" (*Ibid*).

At that instant, Augustine felt a flood of tears welling up to his eyes. To keep his friend from witnessing it, he turned away from him and went into the garden. He needed to be alone, even though Alypius was his alter ego. Alypius understood and did not follow.

Take and read! Take and read!

Emotionally exhausted, Augustine threw himself on the grass under a fig tree and wept bitterly. He began to pray as he had never prayed before:

"And much I said not in these words but to this effect: 'And You, O Lord, how long? How long, Lord; will You be angry forever? Remember not our former iniquities.' For I felt that I was still bound by them. And I continued my miserable complaining: 'How long, how long shall I go on saying tomorrow and again tomorrow? Why not now, why not have an end to my uncleanness this very hour?'" (*Confessions,* Book Eight, XII, p. 178)

Suddenly, as he was praying, he heard a voice from some nearby house, as though that of a boy or girl, repeating in sing-song fashion: "Take and read! Take and read!"

Although somewhat startled by these words, he wondered if there were some child's game in which these words were used. He could think of none. Then, holding back his tears he began to ask himself if perhaps these words were not addressed to him personally in answer to his prayers. Perhaps he was being told to look into the Scriptures and read!

So Augustine hastened back to where Alypius was waiting, for it was there he had laid down his copy of St. Paul's *Epistles.* Opening the book at random, his eyes fell on the following passage, which he began to read in silence:

"Let us live honorably as in daylight; not in carousing and drunkenness, not in sexual excess and lust, not in quarreling and jealousy. Rather, put on the Lord Jesus Christ and make no provision for the desires of the flesh" (Romans 13:13-14).

He read no further. As he himself has said, he had no need to:

"For in that instant, with the very ending of the sentence, it was as though a light of utter confidence

shone in all my heart, and all the darkness of un-
certainty vanished away" (*Confessions*, Book Eight,
XII, p. 179).

Yes, these things had been written for him. A
sudden calm filled his whole being. Later on he
would realize this was a sure sign of God's presence.
All the mystics through the ages have commented
on this phenomenon. Setting down the book and
putting some marker at the place, he told his friend
Alypius all that had been happening to him, and his
face reflected his great peace of soul.

Alypius asked to read the passage himself, and
Augustine showed him the passage. Alypius went
on to read a little further, and pointed out that the
text said: "Extend a kind of welcome to those who
are weak in faith" (Romans 14:1).

Although the humble Alypius applied these
words to himself, Augustine saw in them an encouragement to his own faith. He was totally transformed.
It was a true conversion, almost as memorable in
its own way as Paul's on the road to Damascus.

Monica's joy

Augustine comments: *"Then we went in to my
mother and told her, to her great joy."*

Monica certainly had a right to be the first to
hear the news, for she had been looking forward
to this day for so many years. If she wept now, it
was out of her immense love and gratitude toward
her God. Yes, she had put her trust in prayer. She
had believed that in the end prayers are always answered, even when God makes us wait a long time.

Now Monica discovered that God does not meas-
ure out his favors and graces with a dropper, at least
not to those souls who have earned His munificence
by their perseverance and stubborn insistence.

Without even suspecting to what heights her
Augustine would rise or the great influence he would

have over future generations, she had, that very day, the consolation of understanding what had happened to him. By an astonishing miracle, Augustine now thought only of God and wanted only to serve Him. Even the honorable marriage that had been arranged for him no longer held any attraction. As soon as he was baptized he wanted to devote himself solely to contemplation, after the example of the Egyptian hermits.

We can imagine the elation in Augustine's encounter with his mother when he came with Alypius to tell her: "It's all decided! I don't want to wait any more! I want only to tell God: 'O Lord! I am Your servant, the son of Your handmaid!'"

Throughout his life Augustine would continue to witness to his mother. In his book *De Ordine* ("On Order"), he wrote:

"It is to my mother's prayers that I most certainly owe, as I believe and confirm, the spirit that God has given me, by virtue of which I set nothing above the search for truth, want nothing, think of nothing, and love nothing except the truth."

Augustine has given us some idea of his mother's joyful gratitude to God:

"She was filled with triumphant exultation, and praised You who are mighty beyond what we ask or conceive: for she saw that You had given her more than with all her pitiful weeping she had ever asked. For You converted me to Yourself so that I no longer sought a wife nor any of this world's promises, but stood upon that same rule of faith in which You had shown me to her so many years before. Thus You changed her mourning into joy, a joy far richer than she had thought to wish, a joy much dearer and purer than she had thought to find in grandchildren of my flesh" (*Confessions*, Book Eight, XII, p.179).

Monica had attained her heart's dearest wish. From that moment on, her prayer to God was: "I ask nothing more of life! O Lord, take me whenever You wish!"

There were still several steps necessary to bring the great event of Augustine's conversion to its term. Augustine had to give his life a new direction and prepare himself to receive the wonderful graces of baptism. That was why baptism was then called *regeneration*, that is, a second birth, the beginning of a new life.

Renouncements

Monica immediately noticed the profound change that had occurred in her son. He was a different man. Now he spoke only of retreat, solitude, recollection before God in meditation and prayer. His profession as a teacher of rhetoric now weighed on him. All the earthly ambitions that he might have entertained had disappeared without a trace. He later wrote:

"How lovely I suddenly found it to be free from the loveliness of those vanities, so that now it was a joy to renounce what I had been so afraid to lose. For You cast them out of me, O true and supreme Loveliness; You cast them out of me and took their place in me, You who are sweeter than all pleasure, yet not to flesh and blood; brighter than all light, yet deeper within than any secret; loftier than all honor, but not to those who are lofty to themselves. Now my mind was free from the cares that had gnawed it, from aspiring and getting and weltering in filth and rubbing the scab of lust. And I talked with You as friends talk, my glory and my riches and my salvation, my Lord God" (*Confessions*, Book Nine, I, p. 183).

Monica shared in her son's elation. But there was need to take some practical steps. Augustine wanted silence around him. His conversion had taken place toward the end of August in the year 386, about twenty days before the "Vintage Vacation" which began on September 16th. So the great event must have occurred around August 28th. And on the 28th of August forty-four years later, in 430, God would call him to Himself.

Augustine did not know he still had forty-four years to live, but he was rearranging his life so that every instant of his time should belong to his God. In order not to arouse undue attention, he decided to complete the current school year. Only twenty more days! Should he not make this final effort, so as to retire without noise or fanfare? After carefully weighing the matter, this is the course he decided on, and his mother concurred.

In the next chapter we shall see how Augustine organized his new life while preparing for the great day of his baptism. According to the customs of that time, he could not be baptized—except in an emergency such as the danger of death—before Holy Saturday of the following year, April 24, 387.

Augustine still had eight months before his baptism. God sent him the necessary help to proceed wisely. First of all, he had to finish the school year, and would not be free until September 16th. Those twenty days seemed like a century to him. After that, he would have to follow the course of instruction for catechumens in Milan. These instructions preceding baptism started at the beginning of Lent. So he would have to wait until March, 387.

Meanwhile, the opportunity was provided him to spend the next six months in prayer and meditation.

11

At
Cassiciacum

A house
in the country

As we have already
seen, Monica and Augus-
tine had many generous
friends. This is an im-
portant point for us to
remember. To have so
many friends, they them-
selves must have had a
great capacity for love
and friendship. Mon-
ica's kindness and ser-
vice to others was well
known. As for Augustine,
there was something
about his person, his
way of speaking and act-
ing, that had an indefin-
able yet irresistible
charm. His fellow-towns-
men at Tagaste had
great admiration for
him. At Carthage too
he made close friends.
In their fidelity, they
followed him from Af-
rica to Rome, and then
to Milan.

So Augustine was sur-
rounded by quite a large
number of young men
who thought so much of
him that they even tried

to imitate his words and gestures. He had once led some of them into Manichaeism, and now he was leading them toward the true Faith. Among his friends, Alypius was the closest. This quiet and profound man would some day become a bishop in Africa. But there were others, including Romanianus, who had once placed his vast fortune at the service of Monica and Augustine and entrusted his son Licentius to their care.

As it happened, Romanianus was pleading an important case before the imperial court of Milan. Once again, he placed himself at Augustine's service, to provide for his daily living expenses.

Even before Augustine's definitive conversion, when he was still under the spell of the Platonic doctrines, he and Romanianus had talked of organizing a small, informal college of sorts. It would have been limited to about ten members, dedicated to the study of philosophy and living a retired life in which they would share material things in common. However this project had failed to materialize because several of the proposed members were married and there was no provision for their families in the envisioned scheme of things.

Given his new spiritual horizons, it was natural that Augustine should turn once more to that earlier plan, but with loftier sights than before. First, a secluded place in the country had to be found where several men could live a common life of contemplation. One of Augustine's friends, who was also a teacher of literature, offered him the use of his villa at a place called Cassiciacum, not far from Milan.

The Romans used the term "villa" to refer to a country estate with a master's residence that was large and commodious, although in no sense a castle or château. In addition to the private quarters, the manor house had spacious halls, baths, a library, porticoes, balconies, shaded terraces, space, air, and light.

It was in such a manor house that Monica came to live with her son. We know that it must have been very large because of the number of persons who joined them there.

The guests at Cassiciacum

First of all, Monica came not only as Augustine's mother and the mother of his brother Navigius, but as the foster-mother of all their friends gathered there.

In addition to Monica and Augustine, there was Adeodatus, Augustine's young son. He was now fifteen. Speaking of him, his father later wrote: "We also brought with us the boy Adeodatus.... You had made him well [O Lord]. He was barely fifteen, yet he was more intelligent than many a grave and learned man.... His great intelligence filled me with a kind of awe: and who but You could be the maker of things so wonderful?" (*Confessions*, Book Nine, VI, p. 192)

Augustine now referred to his son Adeodatus as "begotten by me in my sin." Yet he could not deny the precocious genius that exuded from him. To his natural gifts were added an extraordinary innocence, purity, and piety. As proof of this, we have the following anecdote. One day there was discussion as to what sort of a person truly had God within him. Adeodatus quickly answered: "The one who lives in chastity!" And when Augustine asked if by chastity he meant simply avoiding the contrary vices, he explained: "Oh no! A soul is truly chaste only if it constantly keeps its gaze fixed on God and cleaves to Him alone!"

At that time, Adeodatus had not yet been baptized but was preparing for baptism with his father. Great things could certainly be expected from this child. Sadly, he did not live very long, dying shortly after his baptism. Speaking of him in his *Confessions*, Augustine later wrote:

"You took him early from this earth, and I think of him utterly without anxiety, for there is nothing in his boyhood or youth or anywhere in him to cause me to fear" (Book Nine, VI, p. 192).

After Monica, Augustine, and Adeodatus, we must mention the timid and modest Navigius, Monica's second son. He had long since been baptized. At that time he was probably about thirty years old. He was frail, and his only desire was to pray and meditate in silence.

Alypius was the fifth guest at the villa. Although not a blood relative, Augustine loved to call him "my heart's brother." He had shared in Augustine's errors, without however imitating his sexual excesses. For after a few unfortunate experiences he had settled down to a life of perfect chastity, and would not hear of getting married. He, too, was preparing for baptism. He was Augustine's constant confidant and inseparable friend.

Two more names should be added to the list. First, there was Licentius, the son of Romanianus, who had so long befriended Augustine. Licentius was a fiery young man, sometimes lacking in calm and balance. He had a passion for poetry, and composed verses even at table. He was an enthusiast for the classical masterpieces, sang songs of Sophocles, and wept when he read Virgil. On the other hand, he was less interested in philosophy, and had practically no interest in religion.

In gratitude to Romanianus, Augustine wanted to keep him with his group, instruct him, and elevate his sights. However, he was not as successful as he would have hoped in these efforts.

Finally, there was another of Augustine's students, Trigetius, a youth of twenty, and a lover of literature. He had already shown himself to be serious and intelligent. He, too, was preparing for baptism and would be baptized with Augustine.

So far, we have named seven persons dwelling at the villa of Cassiciacum. There were apparently two others about whom we know nothing except that they were cousins of Augustine, Rusticus and Lastidianus by name.

As we can see, Monica, the only woman in the group, must have been kept busy holding the reins and running the house smoothly. She was an efficient woman, and nothing escaped her attention. Augustine has given her homage:

"She took care of us as if we had all been her own children, and she waited on us as if each one of us had been her father!"

The activities at Cassiciacum

What did everyone do at Cassiciacum? Far be it from us to imply that this was primarily a place to relax and enjoy the countryside. As we have already said, Augustine had committed himself to the contemplative life. For it was the example of the Egyptian monks that had finally brought about his conversion. He envied them and wanted to live like them, always offering praise to God. To this end, he had brought with him the sacred book of the Scriptures to read — a book he had too long neglected, as we know. Now he devoted himself entirely to the reading of Scripture, without forgetting the thoughts of the great philosophers.

Before leaving Milan he had sent Bishop Ambrose a message, asking which portion of the Scriptures he should study most carefully. Ambrose had answered that he should delve into Isaiah. For to his mind this great prophet was the principal herald of the Messiah's glorious mission.

Augustine obeyed, but soon discovered he was still too ignorant of the history of Israel to understand Isaiah. Probably at the suggestion of his mother, he opened the Book of the Psalms, with which he was not yet familiar. The Psalms had been the prayer book of the ancients. And nothing could have proved more useful to Augustine at this stage of his life. These great poems dazzled his mind and heart from the start. He would continue to be a passionate admirer of the Psalms throughout his life. Later on, when he was a bishop, the Psalms would be one of the most frequent themes of his sermons to his people — truly a theme with inexhaustible possibilities.

Monica had always been a devotee of the Psalms. She saw them as an inspired collection of man's every aspiration and cry to his God.

Let us reread the passages in the *Confessions* in which Augustine talks to us about the Psalms:

"When I read the Psalms of David, songs of faithfulness and devotion in which the spirit of pride has no entry, what cries did I utter to You, O my God, I but a novice in Your true love, a catechumen keeping holiday in a country house with that other catechumen Alypius: though my mother also was with us, a woman in sex, with the faith of a man, with the serenity of great age, the love of a mother, the piety of a Christian" (Book Nine, IV, p. 188).

It was Monica who guided Augustine and Alypius in reading the Psalms:

"What cries did I utter to You in those Psalms and how was I inflamed towards You by them, and on fire to set them sounding through all the world, if I could, against the pride of man! But in truth they are already sung throughout the world and there is none who can hide himself from Your heat.... I was in in fear and horror, and again I was on fire with hope and exultation in Your mercy, O Father....

"All these things I read and was on fire; nor could I find what could be done with those deaf and dead, of whom indeed I had myself been one for I had been a scourge, a blind raging snarler against the Scriptures, which are all honeyed with the honey of heaven and all luminous with Your light: and now I was fretting my heart out over the enemies of these same Scriptures. When shall I recall and set down all that belongs to those days in the country?" (Confessions, Book Nine, IV, p. 191)

Colloquies

It was especially in the morning that Monica, Augustine, and Alypius read and recited the Psalms. Perhaps other guests at the villa joined with them in singing God's praises. But Augustine's heart was so filled with noble desires and his mind so engrossed with great thoughts that he could not keep them to himself. He was by vocation a spiritual guide and teacher. And so he would gather his young friends around him to comment to them upon the works of Virgil, or to reread *Hortensius*. Even more frequently he would initiate some sort of philosophical colloquy on a lofty subject. We know that during his stay at Cassiciacum he wrote at least a few of his treatises.

Among these treatises is one entitled *"De beata vita"—On the Happy Life.* One of his fundamental notions was that man is created for happiness, and consequently there is nothing more important than to know in what happiness consists and how to attain it. This was one of his favorite subjects. The reason we refer to it is that when he recorded his discussions at Cassiciacum on happiness, he gave special honor to his mother.

Monica is shown to us in an unexpected light in Augustine's *"De beata vita."* Not only was she a devout woman who attended church regularly, prayed much, and knew the Psalms by heart as was the custom. She also had a keen mind and could hold her own in a philosophical discussion. She had received no formal training in this field, but had developed an understanding of it from listening to her son. Augustine presents her to us as a woman of sound judgment, quick perception, and penetrating insights.

The discussions were led by Augustine, as his mother and friends clustered around him. One day he asked: "Tell me, who is the happiest man? Is it not the one who has everything he desires?"

Monica was quick to answer:

"Oh no! If he desires what is good and has it, that is fine. Then indeed he is happy. But if he wants what is evil, even if he obtains it, how can he help but be unhappy?"

With a smile filled with emotion, Augustine cried out:

"O my mother! You have just touched one of the highest summits of philosophy!"

Augustine had good reason to know that a man cannot be happy when he is doing evil things. But he hastened to cite a beautiful passage from *Hortensius* which reached the same conclusion:

"To desire evil is the height of misery. And one is less unhappy not having what one desires than in desiring something evil!"

Monica immediately began to comment on these words in such a felicitous way that, Augustine tells us, her hearers thought they were listening to a great man sitting in their midst. "As for me," he writes, "I contemplated with delight the divine source from which so many beautiful thoughts flowed."

But Monica said even more astonishing things.

The discussion continued on the very human subject of happiness. Augustine declared it is impossible to be happy when one fears to lose this happiness. Everything that comes to an end makes us fearful. And so, Augustine concluded: "Anyone who loves and possesses perishable goods can never be happy."

Monica rejoined:

"Probably not. But I go still further. Even if it were certain they would never be lost, I would still consider such a person unhappy, because everything that is passing is incommensurate with the soul of man. And the more he seeks such goods, the more miserable and indigent he will be."

Augustine objected:

"What's this? If he had all earthly goods in abundance, if, in addition, he knew how to limit his desires, and if he learned the art of enjoying life's pleasures with dignity and moderation, would he not be happy?"

Monica replied:

"No, no! All the goods of this earth will never make a soul happy!"

Augustine was delighted:

"What a beautiful answer! Yes, if anyone wants to be happy, he must rise above perishable things, he must seek something that will remain forever and that can never be snatched away by reverses of fortune. Now, only God is of such a nature, and consequently only in God can true happiness be found!"

The dialogue continued during the following days. Augustine's son proffered answers that rejoiced all present. Then Monica spoke again. She pointed out that God is everywhere, and hence He is also among sinners. But it is not enough to have God within to be happy; we must have Him within us as our friend:

"The person who lives a good life has God within him, but he also has Him as a friend. He who lives an evil life has God within him, but as his enemy. And he who seeks God and has not yet found Him does not yet have God either as a friend or an enemy, for God is still far from him!"

Augustine felt these words did not give sufficient credit to those who are sincerely seeking God. It was as if he anticipated Pascal's beautiful thought: "You would not be seeking me if you had not already found me!" He brought all the discussants to the following conclusion:

"He who seeks God and finds Him has God as his friend, and he is happy. He who is seeking God and has not yet found Him has God as his friend, but he is not yet happy. Finally, he who turns away from God and is driven by his vices to ignore Him is not happy nor does he have God as a friend."

This was the tenor of the conversations among the young guests gathered around Augustine and his mother. Obviously there was nothing frivolous or vulgar about them. They talked only of the highest aspirations of the human soul. And Monica, because she was holy, drew reflections from her own experience that often excelled the answers of the young students Augustine was training in philosophy. It was so evident to everyone that Augustine concluded:

"You can readily see that there is a great difference between those who have studied many books and those who are always closely united to God. For is it not in this intimate union that the soul discovers all the beautiful thoughts we admire in my mother?"

And then he added words whose wisdom summed up his own state of mind at the time:

"Let us think of God, let us seek Him, let us thirst for Him. He is the interior sun that shines within us. And even when our eyes are too weak or so recently opened that they cannot look directly at Him, whatever truth we utter comes from Him alone. Admittedly, as long as we continue to seek, as long as we have not drunk from the wellspring, we must agree we have not yet attained the stage to which we are destined, and are not yet wise or happy. We shall be so only when we know fully with both our minds and hearts: the Father who gives Truth; the Son who is this Truth; and the Holy Spirit, through whom we are joined to the Truth. These Three are seen as One by enlightened souls."

Augustine's words reminded Monica of the sermons of Bishop Ambrose, whom she admired so much, and she spontaneously cried out:

"Blessed Trinity, receive our prayers!"

And as though in a rapture, she added:

"Yes! That is the happy life, the perfect felicity, to which we must aspire with unshakable faith, fervent hope, and burning charity!"

Through meditation in common, through flights of mind and heart, Augustine was being prepared for baptism, together with all those who were to be reborn to Christ with him. His little book *De beata vita* (On the Happy Life) was the fruit of these discussions from which we have briefly quoted. It contains the substance of the conversations on a great variety of subjects that filled those six months spent at Cassiciacum.

Baptism at Milan

The *Confessions* reveal many other aspects of Augustine's life at this period, especially his remorse for the many years he had spent in a life of sin, his great trust in God's mercy, and his humility in confessing to his young friends the misdeeds of his past while beseeching them to pray for him.

By now he had decided to give up the teaching of literature and rhetoric. Before the opening of the 386-387 school year, he wrote to the authorities of Milan stating his decision. The reason he gave for resigning from his post was primarily one of health. His strength had been undermined by the spiritual crises he had been through, his heavy work load, and his deep anxiety for the future. While his friend Alypius gave him a fine example of mortification, he did not yet have the strength to imitate it to the full.

During the winter of 386-387, Augustine tells us he was favored with a miracle of sorts. He had been suffering from a general inflammation that involved his head, teeth, and ears, to the point that he was in constant pain. One day the pain became so acute he thought he could not bear it.

At that very moment the miracle occurred. In his *Confessions* he relates what happened:

"During those days You sent me the torture of toothache, and when it had grown so agonizing that I could not speak, it came into my heart to ask all my friends there present to pray for me to You, the God of every kind of health. I wrote this down on my tablet and gave it to them to read. As soon as we had gone on our knees in all simplicity, the pain went. But what was the pain or how did it go? O my Lord, my God, for as far back as my earliest infancy I had never experienced any such thing. Thus in that depth I recognized the act of Your will, and I gave praise to Your name, rejoicing in faith" (Book Nine, IV, p. 191).

This event proved an added inspiration to love God. From that time on he probably began to say the prayer recorded in the *Confessions,* which expresses his remorse for the time he had wasted and his failure to fulfill his duty to love God:

"Late have I loved You, O Beauty so ancient and so new; late have I loved You! For behold You were within me, and I outside; and I sought You outside and in my unloveliness fell upon those lovely things that You have made. You were with me and I was not with You. I was kept from You by those things, yet had they not been in You, they would not have been at all. You did call and cry to me and break open my deafness; and You did send forth Your beams and shine upon me and chase away my blindness; You did breathe fragrance upon me, and I drew in my breath and do now pant for

You; I tasted You, and now hunger and thirst for You; You did touch me, and I have burned for Your peace" (Book Ten, XXVII, p. 236).

Such were the prayers that welled up from Augustine's heart. His mother rejoiced when she heard them from her son's lips. The days of her sorrow and weeping were over. She was now filled with ecstatic gratitude toward her God. As the time for Augustine's baptism approached, she redoubled her prayers.

It was customary for those who wanted to be baptized at Easter to take special instructions throughout the period of Lent. And so the little colony left the rural delights of Cassiciacum to return to Milan for the beginning of Lent. Augustine could easily have been dispensed from these preliminary catechetical instructions, but he attended the classes diligently, mingling with the ignorant and lowly. It mattered little to him that he had once been a celebrity of sorts in Milan.

It was the year 387. During the night of Holy Saturday, April 24th to 25th, Augustine and his friends bowed before the great Ambrose, as Monica watched, to receive the baptismal water. According to Ambrose, in his treatise *On the Sacraments*, the rite at that time proceeded in the following manner: At a sign from the bishop, the candidate for baptism approached the baptismal font and entered it three times. The first time, he came forth saying: "I believe in God!" The second time, he came out saying: "I believe in Jesus Christ!" And the third time, he said: "I believe in the Holy Spirit!" After this, the bishop would go up to the altar and say a prayer. Then, approaching the neophytes, he poured the sanctifying water on the forehead of each of them, saying: "I baptize you in the name of the Father and of the Son and of the Holy Spirit."

Then Augustine watched the holy bishop bend down before him to wash his feet. After that, he was clothed in a long white linen tunic, the symbol of innocence reconquered by the sacrament of Christ. Finally, holding a lighted candle, he went toward the altar to receive his first Holy Communion.

Who can describe the holy emotions that filled Augustine's heart as well as his mother's during this stirring ceremony? In his book to Honoratus entitled *On the Usefulness of Faith,* Augustine wrote:

"Like a man who has long suffered from thirst and been exhausted by it, I threw myself upon the breasts of Holy Mother Church with all possible eagerness. Bemoaning my wretchedness, weeping over my past, I sucked and pressed them with all my strength to bring forth the milk I needed so desperately in order to recover from my prostration and regain spiritual health and vigor."

For Augustine this was a second birth in the fullest sense of the term. He felt he was a new man. In his *Confessions* he tells how everything in God's temple looked new and different:

"I wept at the beauty of Your hymns and canticles, and was powerfully moved at the sweet sound of Your Church's singing. Those sounds flowed into my ears, and the truth streamed into my heart: so that my feeling of devotion overflowed, and the tears ran from my eyes, and I was happy in them" (Book Nine, VI, p. 193).

We can be sure that Monica shared in her son's ecstatic joy, admiring the effects of grace in his soul and blessing God for the wonderful things He had accomplished in him. She felt she had attained all her desires and fulfilled the purpose of her life.

Plans for the future

Augustine had broken all ties with his past. He had renounced teaching forever. At Cassiciacum he had tasted the greatness of the contemplative life and now wanted only to devote the rest of his life to it. It was easy for him to persuade his close friends to share his aspirations.

But where would they settle down? It seemed obvious they would have to return to Africa, their native land. There they would have the best chance of obtaining the material requirements around which to organize their common life.

As soon as Alypius heard about it, he enthusiastically agreed. Monica, for her part, would always be their common mother, their model, their earthly providence. A young man by the name of

12

Toward a Death of Love

Evodius, also an African, joined the group. It was decided they would return to Carthage and then establish themselves at Tagaste or its immediate environs.

The little party set out for Ostia, the seaport of Rome. There they would not have to wait too long for a ship sailing for Africa.

Before leaving Milan, they must have gone to say farewell to Bishop Ambrose. He in turn must have blessed them and praised their magnificent ambition to become servants of God.

No one had any idea that Monica was approaching the end of her earthly pilgrimage.

Tradition tells us, through the lessons of the Augustinian breviaries, that Monica was then making rapid progress toward the loftiest perfection. Her mind was totally engrossed in God, and she lived in continual union with Him. She never tired of expressing her gratitude for the wonderful favors bestowed on her and her growing desire to see God in the beauty of His eternal light.

The window at Ostia

We have the most graphic description of what was going on in Monica's great soul in Augustine's account of what happened to them when they were already at Ostia, preparing to leave for Africa.

In all of Augustine's immortal *Confessions* there is perhaps no more beautiful passage than the one we might entitle "The Window at Ostia." As we know, the painter Ary Scheffer (1795-1858) has represented the scene in a famous painting.

"When the day was approaching on which she was to depart this life — a day that You knew though we did not — it came about, as I believe by Your secret arrangement, that she and I stood alone leaning in a window, which looked inwards to the garden within the house where we were staying, at Ostia

on the Tiber; for there we were away from everybody, resting for the sea voyage from the weariness
of our long journey by land. There we talked together,
she and I alone, in deep joy; and *forgetting the things
that were behind and looking forward to those that
were before,* we were discussing in the presence of
Truth, which You are, what the eternal life of the
saints could be like, *which eye has not seen nor ear
heard, nor has it entered into the heart of man.* But
with the mouth of our heart we panted for the high
waters of the life which is with You: that being sprin-
kled from that fountain according to our capacity,
we might in some sense meditate upon so great a
matter.

"And our conversation had brought us to this
point, that any pleasure whatsoever of the bodily
senses, in any brightness whatsoever of corporeal
light, seemed to us not worthy of comparison with
the pleasure of that eternal Light, not worthy even
of mention. Rising as our love flamed upward towards that Selfsame, we passed in review the various
levels of bodily things, up to the heavens themselves, whence sun and moon and stars shine upon
this earth. And higher still we soared, thinking in
our minds and speaking and marveling at Your works:
and so we came to our own souls, and went beyond
them to come at last to that region of richness unend-
ing, where You feed Israel forever with the food of
truth: and there life is that Wisdom by which all
things are made, both the things that have been and
the things that are yet to be.

"But this Wisdom itself is not made: it is as it
has ever been, and so it shall be forever: indeed
'has ever been' and 'shall be forever' have no place
in it, but it simply is, for it is eternal: whereas 'to
have been' and 'to be going to be' are not eternal.
And while we were thus talking of His Wisdom and
panting for it, with all the effort of our heart we did
for one instant attain to touch it; then sighing, and

leaving the first fruits of our spirit bound to it, we returned to the sound of our own tongue, in which a word has both beginning and ending. For what is like to Your Word, Our Lord, who abides in Himself forever, yet grows not old and makes all things new!

"So we said: If to any man the tumult of the flesh grew silent, silent the images of earth and sea and air; and if the heavens grew silent, and the very soul grew silent to herself and by not thinking of self mounted beyond self: if all dreams and imagined visions grew silent, and every tongue and every sign and whatsoever is transient—for indeed if any man could hear them, he should hear them saying with one voice: 'We did not make ourselves, but He made us who abides forever': but if, having uttered this and so set us to listening to Him who made them, they all grew silent, and in their silence He alone spoke to us, not by them but by Himself: so that we should hear His word, not by any tongue of flesh nor the voice of an angel nor the sound of thunder nor in the darkness of a parable, but that we should hear Himself whom in all these things we love, should hear Himself and not them; just as we two had but now reached forth and in a flash of the mind attained to touch the eternal Wisdom which abides over all: and if this could continue, and all other visions so different be quite taken away, and this one should so ravish and absorb and wrap the beholder in inward joys that his life should eternally be such as that one moment of understanding for which we had been sighing—would not this be: *Enter you into the joy of your Lord?* But when shall it be? Shall it be when *we shall all rise again* and *shall not all be changed?*

"Such thoughts I uttered, though not in that order or in those actual words; but You know, O Lord, that on that day when we talked of these things the world with all its delights seemed cheap to us in comparison with what we talked of!...." *(Confessions,* Book Nine, X, pp. 199-201)

Detachment

As this amazing contemplation was unfolding and Augustine put its progressive ascents into words, an unexpected change began to take place in Monica's heart. As her son spoke of the vanity of created things, uttering aspirations for eternal love and divine light, the bonds that still held Monica to earthly life seemed to be invisibly loosened. She felt she had no desire for anything, expected nothing more of this earth, and yearned only for her God. She was as though totally lifted above herself by great raptures of love. She was inwardly growing to the lofty stature that God had been preparing for her from all eternity, to the heights of the most sublime holiness.

When Augustine stopped speaking, she spoke the words he has recorded for us and that revealed the newly added beauty of her soul:

"Son, for my own part I no longer find joy in anything in this world. What I am still to do here and why I am here I know not, now that I no longer hope for anything from this world. One thing there was, for which I desired to remain still a little longer in this life, that I should see you a Catholic Christian before I died. This God has granted me in superabundance, in that I now see you His servant to the contempt of all worldly happiness. What then am I doing here?" *(Confessions,* Book Nine, X, p. 201)

We cannot but admire this noble woman's detachment. And it was not a passing attitude. In the days that followed she spoke only of scorn for earthly life and of the happiness of death. She was thinking, of course, of what St. John of the Cross would later call the "death of love." When she died a few days later, her very sickness, as it has been described to us, was simply the languishing love that made her yearn for her God with such intensity that it consumed her body.

Those who were with Monica were astonished, filled with admiration, and really didn't know what to make of her condition. She had often expressed the desire to die in Africa and to be laid to rest in her native soil. But now she made no mention of it because she was totally detached even from this desire. When Alypius, Navigius and the others expressed their surprise, she answered:

"Nothing is far from God, and I have no fear that He will not know at the end of the world from what place He is to raise me up" (*Confessions*, Book Nine, XI, p. 203).

Final illness

Augustine has recorded his mother's death for us. Referring to their contemplative conversation by the window at Ostia, he wrote:

"...within five days or not much longer she fell into a fever. And in her sickness, she one day fainted away and for the moment lost consciousness. We ran to her but she quickly returned to consciousness, and seeing my brother and me standing by her she said as one wondering: 'Where was I?' Then looking closely upon us as we stood wordless in our grief, she said: 'Here you will bury your mother.'

"I stayed silent and checked my weeping. But my brother said something to the effect that he would be happier if she were to die in her own land and not in a strange country. But as she heard this she looked at him anxiously, restraining him with her eye because he savored of earthly things, and then she looked at me and said: 'See the way he talks.' And then she said to us both: 'Lay this body wherever it may be. Let no care of it disturb you: this only I ask of you, that you should remember me at the altar of the Lord wherever you may be.'

"And when she had uttered this wish in such words as she could manage, she fell silent as her sickness took hold of her more strongly....

"And so on the ninth day of her illness, in the fifty-sixth year of her life and the thirty-third of mine, that devout and holy soul was released from the body" *(Confessions,* Book Nine, XI, pp. 201-203).

Tears of sorrow

The moment Monica was dead, her grandson Adeodatus uttered a great cry and threw himself on her body to kiss her for the last time. But Monica's death looked so much like a victory that he was quickly silenced. Everyone knelt around her and tried to pray in silence. But Augustine felt his tears welling up, despite his efforts to hold them back. He rose and approached the bed on which his mother lay, gazed at her for a moment, and with trembling fingers closed the eyes that had shed so many tears for the salvation of his soul. Then he turned away and left the room, not wanting to dampen the joy of this beautiful death by his sobs.

Meanwhile news of Monica's death began to spread. Many Christians of the city hastened to her bier. Augustine and his entourage had only been in Ostia for a few days, but people knew who he was. They had heard about his conversion and about his holy mother Monica.

Clustered around Monica's body, Navigius, Alypius, Adeodatus, and Evodius had begun to recite the Psalms of David aloud. Augustine came and joined them, but he was suffering intensely, as he has told us in his *Confessions:*

"Because I had now lost the great comfort of her, my soul was wounded and my very life torn asunder...I accused the emotion in me as weakness;

and I held in the flood of my grief. It was for the moment a little diminished, but returned with fresh violence, not with any pouring of tears or change of countenance: but I knew what I was crushing down in my heart. I was very much ashamed that these human emotions could have such power over me...and I felt a new grief at my grief and so was afflicted with a twofold sorrow" (Book Nine, XII, p. 204).

The day and the following night were spent in continuous prayer. Then the funeral cortege proceeded to the burial ground. Augustine, pale, silent, crushed with sorrow but holding back his tears, followed the bier. In his *Confessions*, he relates:

"When the body was taken to burial, I went and returned without tears. During the prayers which we poured forth to You when the sacrifice of our redemption was offered for her—while the body, as the custom there is, lay by the grave before it was actually buried—during those prayers I did not weep. Yet all that day I was heavy with grief within and in the trouble of my mind I begged of You in my own fashion to heal my pain; but You would not..." (Book Nine, XII, p. 204).

It was not until the next day that the flood of tears broke. When Augustine awoke he suddenly realized his mother was gone forever. He began to review in his mind all that he owed her, he remembered her gentleness, her deep and enduring affection, her self-sacrifice, and all the menial services she had rendered him for over thirty years. Then, he tells us:

"I no longer tried to check my tears, but let them flow as they would, making them a pillow for my heart:...it was Your ears that heard my weeping, and not the ears of a man, who would have misunderstood my tears and despised them.... I wept for my mother, now dead and departed from my sight, who had wept so many years for me..." (*Confessions*, Book Nine, XII, p. 205).

A son remembers

Augustine would never forget his holy mother. In his *Confessions,* written around the year 400, thirteen years after Monica's death, he expressed the hope that all who would read his book would pray for her. By that time he had, against all expectations, become bishop of Hippo in Africa. After giving the account of her death, he wrote the following words of farewell to her:

"So let her rest in peace, together with her husband, for she had no other before nor after him, but served him, in patience bringing forth fruit for You, and winning him likewise for You. And inspire, O my Lord, my God, inspire Your servants my brethren, Your sons my masters, whom I serve with heart and voice and pen, that as many of them as read this may remember at Your altar Your servant Monica, with Patricius, her husband, by whose bodies You did bring me into this life, though how I know not. May they with loving mind remember these who were my parents in this transitory light, my brethren who serve You as our Father in our Catholic Mother, and those who are to be fellow-citizens with me in the eternal Jerusalem, which Your people sigh for in their pilgrimage from birth until they come there: so that what my mother, at her end, asked of me may be fulfilled more richly in the prayers of so many gained for her by my Confessions than by my prayers alone" (*Confessions,* Book Nine, XIII, pp. 207-208).

Augustine would continue to speak of his mother often in later years. We might cite an example from one of his sermons, delivered thirty years after Monica's death. He wished to warn his people against the superstition that the dead come back to reproach or praise us:

"Oh no! The dead do not come back! For, if this power were given them, I would see my holy mother every single night, my mother who could not live apart from me during her earthly life, who followed me over land and sea even into distant lands, so as not to be separated from me! For, please God, when she entered a better life she did not become less loving and would certainly come to console me when I suffer, for she loved me more than I can ever say!"

Epilogue

At the very start of this book we said that Monica's name is inseparable from her son Augustine's. We said she not only had the privilege of bringing him into the world physically but brought him to the Catholic Faith within which his genius could blossom to maturity as it could never otherwise have done.

Monica was a mother worthy of her son. Augustine, with God's grace, became worthy of so great a mother.

And so our veneration of Monica is part and parcel of the glory we give to St. Augustine. In fact, the cult of Monica came into being as a result of the Church's veneration for one of her most eminent doctors.

However, Monica's name, recorded in the book of the *Confessions* which has been read from generation to generation, was not introduced into any of the early martyrologies, nor in those of Usuard, Bede, Ado or others. Only the religious institutes founded on the Augustinian rule honored Monica before her official canonization by the Holy See.

In the year 1162, a search was begun in Ostia for the bodily remains of St. Monica. A portion of her relics was transported to the French monastery of Arrouaise in the diocese of Arras. It was there that the feast of St. Monica was first celebrated on May 4th.

Much later, toward the end of the reign of Pope Martin V, in 1430, new excavations were begun at Ostia. It was thought Monica's sarcophagus had finally been discovered and the relics were solemnly translated from Ostia to Rome. The body was first placed in the church dedicated to St. Tryphon, then at the insistent request of a famous humanist of the time, Maffeo Vegio, in the church of St. Augustine.

Obviously, the fact that there were two translations of St. Monica's relics, one in 1162 and another in 1430, casts serious doubt on the authenticity of the relics venerated at Rome. This has been explicitly admitted in an article by the Franciscan scholar Emmanuele Romanelli in the *Enciclopedia cattolica*, under the name *Monica*. The Roman Martyrology, in addition to the feast of St. Monica, May 4th, mentions the translation of her relics on April 9, 1430.

The French biographer of St. Monica, Abbé Bougaud, cited with admiration a discourse by Pope Martin V, on the occasion of the transfer of Monica's body to Rome in 1430. In fact he did not hesitate to cite this discourse at length and to hold it up as a sort of Bull of Canonization for St. Monica. However this discourse is now acknowledged to be spurious. It is not known by whom it was written and promulgated.

In 1946 an inscription was found on a tombstone that is certainly St. Monica's grave at Ostia.

But more significant than these uncertain vestiges, we have the pages of St. Augustine's *Confessions* devoted to his mother. Nothing can detract from their emotional power.

Finally, we have the prayer cited earlier which has traditionally been used in the divine office for the feast of St. Monica:

Prayer

"O God, Comforter of the afflicted and salvation of those who hope in You, You mercifully accepted the tears of Blessed Monica for the conversion of her son Augustine. Grant that through the intercession of these two saints, we may weep over our sins and obtain Your forgiveness, through Jesus Christ our Lord. Amen."

BOOKS & MEDIA

The Daughters of St. Paul operate book and media centers at the following addresses. Visit, call or write the one nearest you today, or find us on the World Wide Web, www.pauline.org

CALIFORNIA
3908 Sepulveda Blvd, Culver City, CA 90230   310-397-8676
5945 Balboa Avenue, San Diego, CA 92111   858-565-9181
46 Geary Street, San Francisco, CA 94108   415-781-5180

FLORIDA
145 S.W. 107th Avenue, Miami, FL 33174   305-559-6715

HAWAII
1143 Bishop Street, Honolulu, HI 96813   808-521-2731
Neighbor Islands call: 800-259-8463

ILLINOIS
172 North Michigan Avenue, Chicago, IL 60601   312-346-4228

LOUISIANA
4403 Veterans Memorial Blvd, Metairie, LA 70006   504-887-7631

MASSACHUSETTS
885 Providence Hwy, Dedham, MA 02026   781-326-5385

MISSOURI
9804 Watson Road, St. Louis, MO 63126   314-965-3512

NEW JERSEY
561 U.S. Route 1, Wick Plaza, Edison, NJ 08817   732-572-1200

NEW YORK
150 East 52nd Street, New York, NY 10022   212-754-1110
78 Fort Place, Staten Island, NY 10301   718-447-5071

PENNSYLVANIA
9171-A Roosevelt Blvd, Philadelphia, PA 19114   215-676-9494

SOUTH CAROLINA
243 King Street, Charleston, SC 29401   843-577-0175

TENNESSEE
4811 Poplar Avenue, Memphis, TN 38117   901-761-2987

TEXAS
114 Main Plaza, San Antonio, TX 78205   210-224-8101

VIRGINIA
1025 King Street, Alexandria, VA 22314   703-549-3806

CANADA
3022 Dufferin Street, Toronto, Ontario, Canada M6B 3T5   416-781-9131
1155 Yonge Street, Toronto, Ontario, Canada M4T 1W2   416-934-3440

¡También somos su fuente para libros, videos y música en español!